Sir Hugh Lane
'That Great Picture   g'

HUGH LANE
dublin

Comhairle Cathrach
Bhaile Átha Cliath
Dublin City Council

Sir Hugh Lane
'That Great Pictured Song'

DUBLIN CITY GALLERY THE HUGH LANE

Contents

Berthe Morisot *Jour d'Été*
c. 1879
Oil on canvas, 45.7 x75.2cm
Sir Hugh Lane Bequest, 1917
The National Gallery, London

Director's Foreword

BARBARA DAWSON

On the morning of 7 May 1915, U-boat 20 was on its way home to the German naval base of Wilhelmshaven following its trawl of enemy targets in the Irish seas. Hampered by heavy fog and and running out of fuel, Lieutenant Walther Schwieger was calling it a day. By 1pm, however, the fog had lifted and the passenger steamer *Lusitania*, a flagship of the Cunard Line, came into view. Captain Schwieger fired a torpedo which successfully ripped the beautiful vessel apart, drowning 1,197 passengers and crew, including Sir Hugh Percy Lane. He was thirty-nine years old. A short but brilliant career embodying the opportunities and excitement of the modern age was extinguished.

A climate of revolution swept across Europe at the turn of the twentieth century. Hugh Lane, born in 1875, an ambitious young entrepreneur determined to make his fortune as an art dealer in London, was perfectly placed to be caught up in this environment of new possibilities and beginnings. A shrewd businessman, Lane's career took off while he was still in his early twenties, but, as is usual in the world of buying and selling art, his fortunes regularly dipped and turned. Although appointed director of the National Gallery of Ireland in 1914, Lane continued his business as an art dealer. When he set out for New York on that fateful journey in April 1915 his credit was running out. Before he arrived in the U.S., however, his fortunes had turned around, thanks to his successful sale of paintings to the steel magnate Henry Clay Frick.

When he died, Lane was just a year into his position as Director of the National Gallery of Ireland. Although his passion for art revealed itself early on in his career, it would have been difficult to predict how he was to become a central figure in the birth of Modern Ireland and even harder still to foresee his leaving behind a monumental cultural legacy that is the original collection of the Municipal Gallery of Modern Art as well as an outstanding collection in the National Gallery of Ireland. Despite his young age Hugh Lane made an indelible mark on Irish cultural life which continues to illuminate and inspire research and scholarship as well as ethos and policy.

In *A Speech and Two Poems*, published in 1937, W.B. Yeats recounts his visit to the then Municipal Gallery in 1933. He was very moved to see there paintings and portraits of the people he knew and the events he had witnessed. Looking on these artworks, Yeats speaks of 'the magnificent vitality of her [Ireland's] painters, in the glory of her passions. For the moment I could think of nothing but that Ireland: that great pictured song'.

Through his poetry Yeats gives us a vivid picture of the passion, excitement and controversy that surrounded Hugh Lane's efforts to promote Irish art practice and establish Dublin's Municipal Gallery of Modern Art. The Gallery first opened to the public in 1908 and attracted great praise and attention internationally for its ethos and its collections.

Hugh Lane almost singlehandedly brought forward a distinct identity for Irish art. He commissioned work from Irish artists; he collected Irish art and, for the first time in a public gallery, hung contemporary Irish art alongside its European peers. As part of the Irish Pavilion at the World Fair at St Louis in 1904, he planned an ambitious exhibition of Irish art. His plan was ultimately thwarted by the Department of Agriculture and Technical Studies, who were suspicious of Lane and alarmed by the possible costs of the venture. It was such a missed opportunity to promote Irish art in the US, as Jack B. Yeats ruefully commented. However, the indefatigable Lane went on to organise the exhibition in London in the Guildhall. Thanks to the support of A.G. Temple, Director of the Guildhall, Irish art had its first exhibition abroad in 1904, with over 80,000 people visiting during the three month period.

Hugh Lane's reputation could lie solely in the controversy around the disputed thirty-nine paintings known as the Sir Hugh Lane Bequest 1917 which are shared with the National Gallery London. But, while the issue of ownership has indeed yet to be resolved, Hugh Lane's reach goes beyond this very high profile controversy. During his stellar and short-lived career he influenced so many aspects of cultural life, not only in Ireland and Britain but also internationally. His story has been written several times, his life immortalised in Yeats's poetry and his ambitions embedded in Dublin's City Gallery which now bears his name. It also has the responsibility to continue his work in engendering a continuous and progressive support of visual arts practice and embedding an appreciation of it in the lives of us all. It is tempting to think of how the story would have continued if the fog hadn't lifted that fateful day in May 1915.

All of the contributors to this publication have presented significant new research on a fascinating period of Irish history which allows for critical reflection and a greater understanding of an intriguing, unlikely but profoundly influential protagonist of cultural revolution in Ireland – Sir Hugh Lane. My thanks to all of them for sharing their research and knowledge and to Jessica O'Donnell for co-editing this publication.

John Singer Sargent *Portrait of Sir Hugh Lane*
1906
Oil on canvas, 74.3 x 62.2 cm
Lane Bequest, 1913

"That Great Pictured Song": Hugh Lane's artistic vision for Ireland, a hundred years on

ROY FOSTER

In this time of commemorations, we celebrate the art collector, dealer and gallery founder Hugh Lane who died exactly a century ago, when the RMS *Lusitania* was torpedoed.

My title comes from a reflection of the poet W.B. Yeats who, after visiting the Dublin Municipal Art Gallery (now called Dublin City Gallery The Hugh Lane) in 1937, produced *The Municipal Gallery Revisited*, a canonical poem about the agenda of cultural nationalism which he attributed to himself, Augusta Gregory and J.M. Synge during the years of the Irish Literary Revival around the turn of the century. By 1937 much had intervened, including a revolution and the creation of a new state; Gregory and Synge were dead, and Yeats himself had not long to live.

'For a long time', he recorded, 'I had not visited the Municipal Gallery. I went there a week ago, and was restored to many friends. I sat down after a few minutes, overwhelmed with emotion. There were pictures painted by men, now dead, who were once my intimate friends. There were portraits of my fellow-workers; there was that portrait of Lady Gregory, by Mancini, which John Synge thought the greatest portrait since Rembrandt. [He was wrong, I'm afraid –RF.] There was John Synge himself; there, too, were portraits of our Statesmen, the events of the last twenty years in fine pictures; a peasant ambush, the trial of Roger Casement, a pilgrimage to Lough Derg, event after event; Ireland not as she is displayed in guide book or history, but Ireland seen because of the magnificent vitality of her painters, in the glory of her passions. For the moment I could think of nothing but that Ireland: that great pictured song.'

This powerful surge of feeling would be preserved in *The Municipal Gallery Revisited*:

Heart smitten with emotion I sink down,
My heart recovering with covered eyes;
Wherever I had looked I had looked upon
My permanent or impermanent images:
Augusta Gregory's son; her sister's son,
Hugh Lane, 'onlie begetter' of all these;
Hazel Lavery living and dying, that tale
As though some ballad-singer had sung it all.

For our purposes what is important is that character whom Yeats numbers in his poem: Hugh Lane, 'onlie begetter'. Lane's heritage is in that Municipal Gallery in Parnell Square, Dublin – as it is also, less obviously, in the National Gallery of Ireland in Merrion Square, whose Director he was, and to whom he gifted or bequeathed an astonishing number of works including a key El Greco, Titian's *Portrait of Baldassare Castiglione*, portraits by Sebastiano del Piombo, Bernardo Strozzi, Anthony van Dyck, Paolo Veronese, Francisco Goya, Thomas Gainsborough, William Hogarth, Thomas Lawrence and Joshua Reynolds, landscapes by Claude Lorraine and Jan van Goyen, and what was then thought to be a Rembrandt , *Portrait of a Lady Holding a Glove*.

This munificence suggests a Medici, or a Sainsbury, or certainly someone extremely rich: who poured out gifts with the kind of aristocratic *sprezzatura* that appealed to Yeats. Lane, however, was not like that. He came from a distinctly marginal Irish Protestant-clerical background, with very little money and not much to make his way on – apart from the connections of his mother's sister, Augusta Gregory. Lane's mis-matched parents separated when he was young, his schooling was very sketchy, and he learned what he knew through immersion in the picture-dealing world from a very early age, working as an assistant to Martin Colnaghi and living in a succession of rented rooms in London. The money came and went, which may account for Lane's legendary frugality: like his aunt, he frequently dined on a bun and a piece of fruit and would go out of his way to save a shilling. This continued even after he was knighted in 1909, and bought the lease of the lovely Chelsea house on Cheyne Walk which he filled with treasures. By then he had become a legendary dealer – and less legendarily, collector. These two identities deserve some attention.

We think of Lane above all in connection with French Impressionists, because he is inevitably associated with pictures such as the 'four priceless superstars of the art world' (as the Hugh Lane Gallery website has recently referred to them) by Renoir, Manet, Pissarro and Morisot,

John Butler Yeats
Portrait of William Butler Yeats
c. 1886
Oil on canvas, 76.6 x 64 cm
Lane Gift, 1912

J.B.C. Corot *Landscape Sunset*
1875
Oil on panel, 17.8 x 24.1.cm
Lane Gift, 1912

which are one of the groups of pictures from Lane's collection shared – for exhibition purposes – between the National Gallery in London and the Hugh Lane Gallery in Dublin. They are stunning paintings by any standard, and bear witness to Lane's legendary eye. But in his lifetime, and certainly in the years when he made his name, they weren't the kind of thing he was associated with: his expertise was in Old Masters above all and, as far as French painting went, his personal taste ran rather to Corot, Courbet and the Barbizon School, also heavily represented in the collection he left to the Gallery. Lane's discovery of Impressionism came quite late; his visit to Paris with his friend the painter William Orpen in 1904, where they descended upon the gallery of Paul Durand-Ruel was clearly a key moment.

Claude Monet *Lavacourt Under Snow*
c. 1878-81
Oil on canvas, 59.7 x 80.6 cm
Sir Hugh Lane Bequest, 1917
The National Gallery, London

Lane emerged, more or less, with a few future superstars in his sights. He borrowed twenty paintings from Durand-Ruel to show in Dublin in 1904/05 and brought several to an exhibition of modern art in Belfast in 1906. When Durand-Ruel put on his legendary Grafton Gallery show in London in January 1905, Lane would buy from him Monet's *Lavacourt under Snow* and Manet's *Music in the Tuileries Gardens*; and later, *Eva Gonzalès*, also exhibited in the Grafton show (where in fact Durand-Ruel sold only thirteen paintings but made an influential splash).

In fact, by the time Lane was buying these paintings, Impressionism was well on its way to being 'established', in France, the USA and – just – Great Britain; Manet had been dead over twenty years, after all. I think Lane's personal taste basically stayed with an earlier era; he never took to post-Impressionism, refusing to see Gauguin as anything other than 'barbaric'; and the one Vuillard in his collection, *The Mantelpiece,* though a lovely thing, is more restrained and conventional than the intricately patterned interior studies of figures and textures which make Vuillard the great original he is. Lane bought no Bonnards, though he did buy Puvis de Chavannes, who influenced both Vuillard and Bonnard. Of course, if he had lived beyond 1915 he might have taken to Matisse and Picasso, perhaps persuaded by friends such as John Quinn in New York; but we don't know. He certainly committed himself heavily to Renoir, Degas and their contemporaries, who were commanding enormous prices by 1912.

And he certainly felt that this was the kind of art that should be seen in Dublin. The history of Impressionist collecting in Britain is interesting; while the London avant-garde were well in the swim by the second decade of the twentieth century, with Roger Fry preaching the doctrine of post-Impressionism, at an earlier stage it's interesting to notice how it was Welsh and Scottish collectors who got early into Impressionism – notably the sisters Gwendoline and Margaret Davies in Wales, and the shipping and industrial magnates of Glasgow, buying through the Glasgow dealer Alex Reid: their collecting, and the influence of Impressionism on Scots painters, was the subject of a fascinating exhibition *Impressionism, Scotland and the Art Market* in Edinburgh in 2008. But a certain current of conservatism, not to say philistinism, persisted – and Lane would come up against it in Dublin.

There were all sorts of currents at work. One of Lane's supporters in the cause of bringing the work of French painters to Dublin should have been the writer George Moore – who had been an early admirer of Impressionist painters, having discovered them when he lived in Paris as a young man; he was himself painted – wonderfully – by Manet.

When Yeats later described Moore as a young man in Paris, frequenting the company of artists, 'a man carved out of a turnip, looking out of astonished eyes', I'm sure he was thinking of this picture. Lane enlisted Moore as one of the people who would convince Dublin opinion that the country needed the kind of paintings shown in the Staats Forbes exhibition (with strategic additions) which he mounted in Dublin in November 1904. Moore was therefore lined up to give a lecture in Dublin in December 1904 about modern painting and the need for it to be exhibited in Dublin. But Moore was congenitally mischievous, contrarian and unreliable: he devoted himself to jeering at the 'dull and commonplace' National Gallery of Ireland (whose Director was in the audience); the idiocy of Dublin taste, which turned down Manets when they could have been had for ten pounds instead of a thousand; and above all the need for artistic shamelessness. Moore, in fact, did as much damage as he could, by identifying the new French painting with moral licentiousness, which he airily said was what Dublin really needed. Artistic codes and conventions existed to be broken, he said, and the point of art was liberation. Dublin needed cafés and a demi-monde rather than a new art gallery: and Ireland needed images of sensual beauty rather than gazing on 'the meagre thighs of dying saints'. 'Life is a rose that withers in the iron fist of dogma, and it was France that forced open the deadly fingers of the ecclesiastic and allowed the rose to bloom again. And France is in the vanguard today in the repudiation of the deadly doctrine that some Bedouin tribe invented in the desert long ago, that life is a mean and contemptible thing, and that renunciation of life is the greatest virtue.'

The painting which Moore took as his leitmotif was the magnificently earthy portrait of *Eva Gonzalès* by Manet, with her splendid arms and independent career as a painter. Moore would recycle this lecture later as a pamphlet; he also read it to a private audience in the painter Philip Wilson Steer's Chelsea studio in May 1906. This was the inspiration for Orpen's wonderful painting *Homage to Manet*. Here Moore is reading from his lecture to an audience which includes Lane, and other arbiters of artistic taste – P.W. Steer, Henry Tonks, Walter Sickert and D.S. McColl – the latter of whom would appear later in Lane's story, as something of a villain.

The last thing Lane needed, however, was for the kind of painting he wanted to bring to Ireland to be identified with an onslaught on dogmatic Catholicism – which is the message that easily shockable people like Edward Martyn and Joseph Holloway took away from Moore's lecture. This flagged up a warning that Lane's campaign to bring

Édouard Manet *Eva Gonzales*
1870
Oil on canvas, 191.1 x 133.4 cm
Sir Hugh Lane Bequest, 1917
The National Gallery, London

modern European art to Ireland, beginning in 1904, was never going to be easy. As is well documented, Lane hadn't shown much interest in his Irish origins before then, and it was only exposure to the circle of his aunt Augusta, Lady Gregory at Coole Park (who didn't at first take to him) that directed his thinking towards Ireland as an appropriate area for cultural entrepreneurship. When Lane put on an exhibition of Old Master Paintings in the RHA with a section featuring 'Irish painters' in 1902, and announced that there were many unknown artistic treasures hidden away in Irish houses, the owners of such houses began to besiege him with requests to sell them. More importantly, Lane entered the world of Dublin movers and shakers including the artist Sarah Purser, and other friends of his aunt's and Yeats's; and quite soon he began advancing the idea of a Gallery of Modern Art for Ireland. This coincided with the exposure of Impressionist painters to a wider British audience, following the Grafton Gallery show. The significance of the new Municipal Gallery he set up in Harcourt Street in January 1908 was potentially immense, as was the art he put into it. In the photographs of its interiors, lovingly arranged by Lane, who was playing to his strengths, you can see not only paintings now familiar to Irish gallery-goers, but also pieces of Irish Georgian furniture which are still in the Hugh Lane Gallery in Dublin. He was possibly influenced by the way Durand-Ruel liked to show paintings, in his own house rather than hung or stacked in a commercial premises. And there is a sense in which Lane, orphaned in several senses, made of the Gallery a house of his own – which sceptics would see as a 'Big House'. The Ascendancy air of the enterprise would be held against it from the start.

It is worth, therefore, setting Lane for a moment against the Ireland of his time. The year when the Municipal Gallery of Modern Art opened in Harcourt Street – 1908 – was a moment of artistic and cultural ferment, and high political hopes. The year before had seen the opening at the Abbey Theatre of Synge's controversial play *The Playboy of the Western World*, with attendant riots; Augustine Birrell had arrived in Dublin as Chief Secretary, and introduced The Irish Council Bill (a sort of Home Rule Bill) which had been rejected by the Irish Parliamentary party; James Larkin had begun organising Dublin dock workers, forming the ITGWU the next year; and the Fenian revolutionary Tom Clarke had returned from America and set up his tobacconist's shop in Dublin in Parnell Street: eight years later he would be one of the chief planners and leaders of the 1916 Easter Rising. The radical collection of pressure groups that made up the Sinn Féin movement were also coalescing into something like a political party

(1908 was the year when they took the formal name Sinn Féin, and contested their first by-election). That year also saw the passing of the Irish Universities Act setting up the National University of Ireland, the foundation of the Irish Women's Franchise League, and the founding of Patrick Pearse's school St Enda's, which would be a sort of madrasa of revolution. The influence of Yeats and Lady Gregory had been asserted over the Abbey, and Yeats was moving away from the radical nationalism of his youth; one knock-on effect was the growth of small agit-prop dramatic companies (one of the most avant-garde, in Hardwicke Street). There was a plethora of radical political and cultural associations springing up. Though the Irish Home Rule party's influence was in the ascendant again at Westminster, with a Liberal government in power and the prospect of Home Rule advancing, Arthur Griffith's Sinn Féin party had established themselves in local politics, notably on urban councils, and were beginning to fight occasional by-elections.

One of the major issues in urban politics was the question of slums and living conditions in the inner city. So when Lane, Purser and various well-connected people agitated for money to purchase modern paintings and a building to house them, there was a predictable groundswell against the idea: modern art was described as a luxury in a city that needed root-and-branch social reform. And thanks to George Moore, a flavour of libertinism and license was also attached to the new painting (as was often mentioned disapprovingly in relation to Renoir's buxom girls in the arms of burly workmen).

Nonetheless, it is interesting that prominent Sinn Feiners like Alderman Tom Kelly became early on convinced supporters of the cause. An impressive commitment was actually made by Dublin Corporation. When Lane masterminded that first exhibition of choice items from the Staats Forbes Collection in November 1904, and various fundraising enterprises began to be prospected among the wealthy, the arguments became heated; but it wasn't a simple question of privilege against radicalism. Perhaps because the great capitalist William Martin Murphy, and the brewing millionaire Lord Ardilaun, were criticised by the Gallery's advocates for their opposition, so Sinn Féin and the Labour movement, represented by the legendary Jim Larkin, weighed in on the Gallery cause. Despite the Ascendancy aura which I have mentioned, the cause became notable for the broad and varied range of its supporters – suggesting, perhaps, an anticipation of a pluralist Ireland under Home Rule. And also, perhaps, an implicit statement that the freedoms of modern art were more attuned to the new Ireland than the puritanical

Antonio Mancini *Lady Gregory*
1906
Oil on canvas, 74 x 57 cm
Lane Gift, 1912

dictates of authoritarian churchmen. Cultural institutions such as the Abbey Theatre, under Lady Gregory's firm direction, contributed to the cause by international tours, and the printing of souvenir items such as an elaborate handkerchief decorated by scenes of plays and star actors.

In the middle of it all, Lane tacked and veered, and took offence, and flounced between Dublin and London. Yeats's pugnacious public poems did little to help. I won't rehearse the ins and outs of it all yet again here; but briefly, when Lane's preferred design, a gallery designed by Lutyens to span the Liffey, was turned down, and debates in the Corporation turned nasty, in 1913, he offered on loan thirty-nine modern paintings to the National Gallery in London. The London gallery accepted them, though with the proviso that they could not yet exhibit them and they eventually let it be known that they didn't think many of them worth hanging, including Renoir's *Les Parapluies*, Monet's *Lavacourt under Snow* and several other stunners. This was one reason for Lane's changing his mind yet again two years later, adding a codicil to his will of 1913 leaving the thirty-nine paintings back to Dublin, if a suitable gallery were built to contain them and other modern paintings of the Municipal Gallery collection.

The other vital change was that in 1914 Lane had become – at last – Director of the National Gallery in Dublin, and had begun energetically to endow it with gifts and plan for the future. This too was not without controversy, as he was still a big-time dealer, and still operating on a knife-edge of debt – especially after the art market collapsed with the advent of war. The years 1914-15 saw him buying back pictures which he had sold to clients who were now in financial difficulties, notably Holbein's great portrait of Thomas Cromwell and Titian's *Man in a Red Hat*. In fact, Lane was on the edge of having his debts called in (he already owed £30,000 before spending a similar sum on paintings at this time). But in a great coup, he sold both these star paintings to the American multi-millionaire Henry Clay Frick. It was this deal and his debt that necessitated his trip to New York in early 1915, as a independent expert for Lloyds as to the value of damaged paintings, and his fatal return voyage on the *Lusitania*, ending tragically a century ago.

This was, of course, the beginning of another story: the story of the thirty-nine paintings. What did they represent? Well, for a start, a value which was estimated at this time of £60,000: which would escalate sharply as Impressionist values – already high when Lane began buying – soared into the stratosphere. The codicil to Lane's will, found in his desk in Merrion Square, was perfectly clear about his wish to leave them to Dublin; but the handwritten codicil was unwitnessed (though carefully initialled by Lane on every page) and the London Gallery stood on the letter of the law, all the more firmly after they (rather belatedly) exhibited the paintings in 1917. A long wrangle began, not entirely resolved even yet.

But let's look once again at the context of the times. Already in 1915, Ireland had narrowly avoided civil war over Ulster's resistance to Home Rule; the outbreak of World War had acted as a kind of lightning rod, directing militant energy elsewhere, but the country remained an armed camp, with paramilitary preparations continuing covertly on the part of advanced nationalists. Less than a year after Lane's drowning, Dublin erupted in flames in the 1916 Easter Rising. Had the bridge gallery been given the go-ahead back in 1913, it and its contents would have been blown to smithereens by the gunboat *Helga* which came up the Liffey and bombarded the rebel strongholds. In 1918, Sinn Féin would sweep the board in the general election and begin their policy of setting up an alternative parliament in Ireland, Dáil Eireann which would increasingly be backed up by the Army of the Irish Republic (or IRA), as the dissident Volunteers now called themselves. From early 1919, the country would become convulsed by guerilla war. The conditions of Ireland, and the bitterness of Anglo-Irish relations, from 1916 to 1922, are the inescapable background to the campaign mounted by the Friends of the National Collections of Ireland to get the pictures back. It would have been very different if, as Lane expected to happen, a Home Rule Ireland had come into being (though this is to assume a number of known unknowns).

Nonetheless, the campaign did get going and the point to stress is how extraordinarily it bridged the chasms opening up in Irish life – between Ulster and nationalist Ireland, between labour and capital, between Ascendancy and demos. Thomas Bodkin puts it well:

> Never before and probably never again in the history of Ireland will our people be found in such absolute unanimity on any question. At one time or another Arthur Griffith, General Michael Collins, President Cosgrave, Mr de Valera, Mr John Redmond, Lord Carson, Lord Craigavon, Protestant and Catholic bishops, the Moderator of the General Assembly of the Presbyterian Church, Unionists, nationalists, Sinn Féiners, judges and generals, peers and proletarians, artists, scholars and professionals and businessmen, rich and poor, have found themselves together working for the same end.

Above all, the campaign to regain the paintings became the central cause of Augusta Gregory's life – and she determinedly kept agitating, string-pulling, visiting, lecturing, writing pamphlets, and desperately hoping, until her death in 1932. Her pamphlet 'Case for the return of the Lane Pictures' remains one of the most succinct and devastating cases for the return of the paintings to Ireland, and an exposé of the distinctly threadbare, self-interested and illogical reasons put forward for retaining them in Britain. A commission to look into the matter unequivocally admitted that Lane's intention had been to leave them to Ireland, but speculated that, had he lived to see the extension to the Tate Gallery paid for by Lord Duveen, where the paintings were to be hung, he would have changed his mind; with a 'rider' argument that the expense of the building, and Duveen's understanding that the Lane paintings were to grace it, presented a kind of moral onus on the National Gallery to keep them. This occasioned Yeats's famous quip, that it was as if Ali Baba and the forty thieves claimed that they had a moral right to the stolen treasure because they had gone to the expense of digging a cavern to hide it. Other more relevant might-have-beens, such as the fact that soldiers who died in action didn't have to have their wills witnessed, or that Scottish law didn't require a witness signature to a codicil, were ignored; and people who had been favourable to Lane's endeavours for Dublin now changed sides and supported London's claims. Further arguments were presented from the Dublin side supported right across the Irish (and Northern Irish) political spectrum: all Irish opinion united in seeing the London Gallery's (and the British government's) attitude as indefensible and unethical. But they remained immoveable.

Over the years, various attempts have been made to share the pictures – an approach floated early on, but initially rejected by the Irish side as appearing to accept that Lane's codicil had no force, whereas even the British side agreed that it had moral force. In 1959 a welcome advance was made, by the initiation of an amicable sharing arrangement, brokered by Lord Longford and Lord Moyne and probably Sir Denis Mahon, to make the pictures available to 'the people of Ireland' (occasioning some nice cartoons in that valuable journal *Dublin Opinion*). Further revisions eventually left thirty-one of the paintings more or less permanently in Dublin – those paintings which had not, it might be said, stood the test of time, like poor old Mancini – while the eight masterworks (all now of huge monetary value) were divided into two sets of four, swapped back and forth across the Irish Sea.

Recently, I went, like Yeats, to a gallery to look at pictures. It was the Sainsbury Wing of the great National Gallery in Trafalgar Square, to see the exhibition *Inventing Impressionism: Paul Durand-Ruel and the Modern Art Market* – a fascinating profile of the man (and indeed the dynasty) who had so much to do with presenting Impressionism to the world. The climactic room at the end is called 'Impressionism's Triumph: London 1905' and it brings together several of the works exhibited by Durand-Ruel at the Grafton Galleries in 1905. This was the show that highlighted how behind-hand English collections were in acquiring Impressionist paintings that now looked like undisputed masterpieces, including Monet's *Lavacourt under Snow*, Manet's *Music in the Tuileries Gardens*, and dominating the room – as she always does – the same artist's *Eva Gonzalès*. In the exhibition devoted to Durand-Ruel's influence, now hanging in Trafalgar Square, the legend beside each painting – the Monet of Lavacourt and the two great Manets – carries, as its location and owner, 'National Gallery, London'. The Monet has the additional catalogue information that the French Impressionist Fund planned to present this painting to the Gallery in 1905, but was told it would not be acceptable: 'by a twist of fate', the catalogue adds, 'the Monet entered the Gallery collection in 1917 as part of the Sir Hugh Lane Bequest'.

A 'twist of fate', indeed, is one way of putting it. But I can think of others. I don't think it is unreasonable for me – or for anyone who has studied the history of the Lane paintings – to feel a glow of righteous rage when we see the ownership of these paintings vested solely and simply in the National Gallery, London. The arguments in favour of that vested ownership are no more convincing than they ever were; it was even implied to me by a former Director of the London Gallery that Dublin didn't really have the resources to display them properly, an argument eloquently contradicted by the marvellous extension to the Hugh Lane Gallery in Dublin. The paintings can and should be lent and shared (as many more great works of art should be) between the galleries of our two countries: appropriately so, at a time when relations between the two countries have never been better, when recent years have seen the astonishingly successful (and moving) first state visits of a British monarch to the Republic of Ireland, and an Irish president to the United Kingdom; and when, in the commemoration of World War I, the British and Irish heads of state together inaugurated a memorial to the war dead of both nations. This publication is also a gesture of commemoration, of Hugh Lane's vision and his wishes, so clearly outlined at the time of his death a hundred years ago.

In a comprehensive survey of the story of Lane and his pictures published in 1932, Lane's friend and successor as Director of the National Gallery of Ireland Thomas Bodkin wrote, 'Only the English people can provide the desirable happy ending'. Surely, in commemorating this decade of anniversaries of the Irish revolution in which we are immersed, a symbolic act of restitution might be made, and ownership of all thirty-nine Lane paintings vested in the Gallery that bears his name (while still shared, for purposes of exhibition, between London and Dublin). They are part of that 'great pictured song' by which Yeats envisioned Irish history. That song includes a litany of injustices now passed into history and past redressing – 'things we wish had not happened', as Queen Elizabeth herself remarked after her visit to the Garden of Remembrance, dedicated to executed Irish revolutionaries, just across the road from the Hugh Lane Gallery. But by acknowledgement of the true ownership of the Lane pictures, however belatedly, a long-standing historical injustice might actually be righted, and thus, in time, forgotten – which is surely the best way to commemorate history.

This text was first delivered at the Hugh Lane Gallery on the centenary of the sinking of the *Lusitania* on 7 May 2015.

Antonio Mancini *Sir Hugh Lane*
1906
Oil on canvas, 226.1 x 116.8 cm
Lane Bequest, 1913

Hugh Lane: Art Dealer and Collector

ROBERT O'BYRNE

Little in Hugh Lane's background suggested he would become one of the most successful art dealers of his era. Born in 1875, he came from ill-matched parents. His mother Adelaide Persse grew up a member of the landed gentry at Roxborough, County Galway, while his father James Lane was scion of a well-established mercantile family in Cork. Disparate backgrounds were to be the cause of difficulties between the couple but, in addition, Adelaide was six years older than her husband who, immediately prior to their marriage in 1870, had taken orders in the Church of England. Living on a cleric's stipend the couple were never wealthy, their annual income in the region of £450 only once James Lane became incumbent of his own parish in the Cornish town of Redruth in 1877. It was here that Hugh Percy Lane, the third-born of six children to survive to adulthood, was raised, in an area known for copper mining (there were some 350 pits in the vicinity).

Lane's education was patchy and he does not appear ever to have attended school for any length of time: when proposing himself for the directorship of the National Gallery of Ireland in 1914, he admitted his academic skills were almost nonexistent and observed that the only subject for which he had ever shown much aptitude was history. It did not help that Adelaide Lane regularly left her husband and went to stay in a variety of English coastal towns such as Plymouth and Portsmouth, and even as far as Paris, taking the children with her. Thomas Bodkin believed Lane's limited schooling forever after left him with a sense of handicap when it came to being persuasive in either speech or print. On the other hand, his peripatetic and unsettled youth gave him an unusual degree of self-assurance and the ability to rely on personal charm, both of which would be useful once he started working as an art dealer.

That career began in the autumn of 1893 when two circumstances occurred: Lane turned eighteen and his mother sought a formal

William Orpen *Rev. J.W. Lane*
1907
Oil on canvas, 91.4 x 78.7 cm
Presented by Sir Alec Martin through the Friends
of the National Collections of Ireland, 1952

Frank Brooks
Portrait of Hugh Lane's Mother, Adelaide Lane
1901
Oil on canvas, 58 x 47 cm
Purchased from David and Alison
Thistlethwaite, 2001

separation from her husband. The already fragmented family life in Cornwall came to an end just at the moment when Lane was old enough to seek employment. Despite possessing no formal qualifications, he had a keen interest in art and had a highly developed visual sensibility. As a boy, he had sometimes helped an elderly woman in Plymouth who cleaned and restored pictures, so this could be posited as some kind of skill. Accordingly, Adelaide Lane turned to her sister Augusta, who had already provided assistance in securing a legal separation from James Lane. Augusta's much older husband Sir William Gregory had died the previous year and, not yet absorbed in Irish literature and the creation of an Irish national theatre, she still spent much of her time moving in London society. It was thanks to connections made through her late husband, who had been a Trustee of the National Gallery London, that Lady Gregory was able to secure Hugh Lane an apprenticeship with one of London's best-known dealers, Martin Colnaghi.

This was an opportune moment to enter the field, as growing numbers of the British landowning classes found their revenues in decline, primarily but not exclusively owing to cheap food imports from the Americas, and at the same time they were expected to pay the new tax of death duties. As a result, many of them were obliged to dispose of assets, not least the treasures accumulated by previous generations. Dealers like Martin Colnaghi, who had his own business, the Marlborough Gallery, at 53 Pall Mall, London, were perfectly placed to assist in the transfer of art from one group of owners to another. Colnaghi believed the best way to learn about art was not through reading books but by directly examining the work, and this was just one of many lessons he passed on to his new employee. Likewise, his own area of expertise was Dutch and Flemish paintings of the seventeenth century, and this was also to be the case with Lane. But Colnaghi's reach was broad: one of his greatest coups was buying a Raphael from the Earl of Ashburnham for £17,000; it was subsequently bought by the American millionaire J.P. Morgan for £80,000. Hugh Lane would enjoy many similar results from his own picture dealing.

Colnaghi and Lane ought to have enjoyed a happy relationship but master and apprentice soon clashed. It would appear the new member of staff wanted to move too fast for his employer who was more than half a century older and settled in his ways. Lane was ambitious to learn and to be in charge, especially once he had observed what money there was to make in picture dealing. For this reason, less than a year after taking up a position with the Marlborough Gallery he left to strike out on his own.

This was an extremely brave move for a nineteen-year-old with little education and few advantageous contacts, other than his aunt Augusta, who by this time had grown irritated with his failure to appreciate her help and what she perceived to be his snobbishness. Nevertheless, by dint of hard work and careful study Lane fast developed a reputation within his chosen trade. Following the example of Colnaghi, he honed his eye by scrutinizing every picture encountered: diaries he kept while on frugal expeditions to mainland Europe indicate that the greater part of his time was spent assiduously visiting churches and museums, and making notes on the paintings found therein. The result of this combination of diligence and industry was that, by the time he had turned twenty-one, Lane's standing in the art world was sufficiently high for him to be invited to go into partnership with another established dealer, E. Trevelyan Turner, who worked from premises at 46 Pall Mall. Here Lane, who had to borrow £800 from his mother in order to buy a share in the company, assumed responsibility for buying Old Masters. However, as had been the case before, relations with his colleague soon began to sour, a situation not helped by the discovery that Trevelyan Turner was taking money from

Rose Barton *Lindsey House from the River*
Watercolour on paper, 36.8 x 26.8 cm
Presented by the artist in remembrance of Sir Hugh Lane

the business to pay personal debts, and that pictures Lane had acquired were being sold without his receiving any recompense. Finally, when he found his salary going unpaid, he sued the senior partner and left, never again to work for or with someone else. Instead, in February 1898 he opened his own establishment, just a single room, at 2 Pall Mall Place. Here he sat on his own each day, able to afford new stock only once he had sold work already acquired. Lady Gregory would later remember an occasion when, after taking a break from his little gallery to meet some cousins, Lane discovered on his return that he had missed a potentially important client, London's Lord Mayor.

Extant diaries from this period show him perforce avoiding all extravagance: when abroad, for example, he carried his own luggage to avoid the price of a porter and would diligently hunt for the cheapest hotel room. He was equally abstemious when it came to spending money on food, a habit that remained with him for the rest of his life. William Orpen called Lane 'the meanest man to himself I have ever known. No matter how tired he was, if he had the time he would walk to save a penny bus fare'. Likewise, a young South African architect Joseph Solomon, in a short memoir written after Lane's death, remembered his friend had told him how, when he was still a young dealer, he would go without meals for several days to save money for the purchase of a picture or sculpture. Forever after, he deemed money spent on lunches and dinners as 'waste', instead smoking plentiful quantities of low-grade and low-price cigarettes. Many people thought poor diet undermined Lane's already precarious health, because he was often unwell, subject to nervous collapses during which he had to take to his bed for days.

Despite, or perhaps because of, his thriftiness, by the time Lane reached his mid-twenties he had become an established dealer in London, making enough from buying and selling pictures to take time off for his other interests (not least the establishment of a municipal gallery in Dublin). Lane once informed Lady Gregory it was deemed a poor year in which he did not make £10,000. Much of this income derived from buying pictures that had been overlooked by other dealers and then selling on the work after it had been cleaned and an attribution confirmed. In June 1901, for example, the National Portrait Gallery in London acquired from Lane an anamorphic painting of the boy-king Edward VI by sixteenth-century Dutch artist William Scrots. The institution paid £100 for this picture; Lane had bought it a year before at auction, when it was catalogued as a portrait of a girl 'in eccentric attitude.' But prior to making the purchase he had examined the picture and noted there were rings on one side so that, when pulled outwards from a wall, the necessary angle of view could be obtained. Furthermore, the reverse was stamped with a crown and initials, indicating the work had been inventoried during the reign of Charles I as part of the British royal collection. Lane paid £8 for the painting; he sold it to the NPG for £100.

Thanks to such astute deals, Alec Martin, a friend who later became managing director of Christie's, described Lane as the finest judge of a picture he had ever met. Likewise, Sir Frederic Burton, the Clare-born artist and Director of the National Gallery in London, told Lady Gregory, 'I have never in all my life been able to have the same courage in my opinion as that young man'. In a posthumous tribute in *The Burlington Magazine*, Henry Tonks wrote that Lane had possessed an extraordinary power to detect a good picture, 'which seemed like a natural gift.' He specialised in recognising the true value of pictures overlooked by others in the trade. A typical instance of this ability to spot 'a sleeper' was demonstrated in the autumn of 1911, when he bought a portrait presumed to be by Sir Thomas Lawrence for £756 at a Christie's auction. Lane questioned the attribution, believing another artist, George Romney, responsible for the picture. A cursory cleaning of the canvas after he had taken it home revealed that his instincts were correct. Romney's portrait of Mrs Edward Taylor is now in the collection of the National Gallery of Ireland.

What made this talent all the more remarkable was Lane's relative inarticulacy when it came to speaking or writing about his area of expertise. He operated in an age during which art scholarship underwent enormous advances thanks to pioneering work by the likes of Wilhelm von Bode in Germany and Bernard Berenson in Italy and, although some of their attributions have since been reassessed, there is no doubt that the adoption of a scientific and academic approach to art revolutionised the study of Old Master painting. This was a skill Lane never acquired, depending instead solely on his intuition and his eye. While other dealers were able to argue an attribution on the grounds of technical details or signature stylistic features, he was obliged to rely on such statements as 'If a painting is beautiful, it is certain it was not painted by a second-rate man'. When a so-called Poussin he had given to Lady Gregory was called into question by another art expert, Lane simply responded, 'That yellow tree is Poussin'. Although there were occasions when doubts were raised about his judgement, and times when indeed he made mistakes, for the most part Lane was rightly accepted as one of the most astute authorities on Old Masters of his generation.

Within a decade of setting up on his own, he was sufficiently wealthy to operate not from commercial premises but from a private residence. Some years after first meeting the painter William Orpen in 1903, Lane shared a room with him in London's South Bolton Gardens, the latter using it as a studio while Lane used it as a storage space/ gallery. Begun in 1906, Orpen's *Homage to Manet* was painted in South Bolton Gardens. Here, behind the figures of Lane, writer George Moore, artists Philip Wilson Steer, Henry Tonks and Walter Sickert, and critic D.S. MacColl, can be seen Manet's portrait of Eva Gonzalès which Lane owned, and another of his belongings, a statue of Venus which would later stand in the first-floor drawing room of the house he bought on Chelsea's Cheyne Walk.

The figures assembled in the picture give an idea of the circles in which Lane moved by this date: it was through his friendship with Orpen, and his campaign for a gallery of modern art in Dublin, that he came to socialise with writers and critics as well as living artists, including John Singer Sargent, who painted his portrait in 1906, Max Beerbohm and John Lavery. At the same time, for reasons of both work and personal inclination, Lane liked to mix with the upper echelons of British and Irish society. As a poor and unknown young man, he had longed to meet members of the aristocracy; Lady Gregory's diaries from this period, when she sometimes took her nephew out to lunch, find her frequently irritated by what she described as his 'second-rate fashionable talk and vulgarity of mind'. There is no doubt that throughout his life Lane was somewhat enamoured of the grand and titled; in December 1909 Augustus John wrote to Lady Ottoline Morrell that Lane – then employing the artist to paint a series of panels for the entrance hall of the house in Chelsea – was 'a silly creature and moreover an unmitigated snob'. He had been thrilled when in June of the same year the King's birthday honours list awarded him a knighthood 'for his services to art'. As Lady Gregory, by now reconciled to her nephew, later explained, this title gave Lane 'a sort of official rank without having to explain what he had done'. Some peers, no doubt, wished to meet him because he might buy paintings from them and thereby ease their financial problems. The beautiful Violet, Duchess of Rutland, a highly talented sculptor, invited him to the family seat of Belvoir Castle where he was expected to examine its picture collection and provide estimates of certain works' value. Soon the Duchess was enquiring whether Lane would be interested in purchasing some paintings. 'They might be of use to you', she suggested, 'and anyhow, you could perhaps very kindly tell me if you thought them very good'. Another friend of similar ilk was Gladys, Marchioness of Ripon, the great supporter of Serge Diaghilev and the Ballets Russes in England. On the occasion of the company's visit to London in 1911 she invited

Lane to dinner with the enticement that 'You will meet Pavlova and various other very interesting people'. He spent weekends at the Ripons' country house, Studley Royal in Yorkshire, and also called on Lady Ripon at her luxurious villa, Coombe Hill in Surrey, where he was asked to give advice on decor; 'I am depressed at yr. having seen my bedroom before it was properly arranged', she wrote to him after one lunch. Perhaps his greatest social coup was becoming close to Queen Victoria's youngest son, Arthur, Duke of Connaught and his Prussian-born wife Princess Louise Margaret. More than once he was invited to stay with the couple at Bagshot Park in Surrey and when their daughter Margaret and her husband, the Crown Prince of Sweden, visited London, the entire family came to him for tea.

Likewise, in Ireland, many of those who Lane numbered among his closest friends and supporters in the campaign to establish Dublin's Municipal Gallery of Modern Art came from the same class as the Duchess of Rutland and the Marchioness of Ripon. Among the first he got to know were the Earl and Countess of Drogheda, who lived at Moore Abbey in Monasterevin, County Kildare, where Lane often stayed, even once spending Christmas there despite the house's reputation for extreme cold. More comfortable, and soon equally well-known to him, was the Earl and Countess of Mayo's home, Palmerstown in Straffan, County Kildare, which offered guests such modern luxuries as private bathrooms and water-closets. Other members of Lane's Irish social circle were Lieutenant Colonel William Hutcheson Pöe of Heywood, County Laois; the Earl of Dunraven from Adare, County Limerick; and Sir Algernon Coote, who lived in great splendour at Ballyfin, County Laois. The magnificence of his house, however, helped to mask the fact that, like so many other aristocrats, Sir Algernon was asset-rich but cash-poor and obliged to dispose of some of his pictures, such as Greuze's *The Capuchin Doll* which he sold to Lane in February 1914 for £800; it is now in the collection of the National Gallery of Ireland.

Mingling in these circles, Lane, although provident at home, was obliged to spend money, not least on his appearance. Standing just below six feet tall, he was slim and somewhat nervous in manner; though charming and persuasive in private company, he could become shy and self-conscious in larger social gatherings. Despite having a rather large nose and ears, he was vain and, while young, rather dandyish, favouring boldly checked waistcoats and jackets. With age, his style of dress grew more sober but he was nevertheless constantly well turned out and invariably exuded an impression of extreme tidiness. It was typical of his attention to detail that the tie and tiepin he wore would be selected to harmonise exactly one with the other. Soon after his appointment as Director of the National Gallery of Ireland in February 1914, he discovered that the holder of this post was entitled to a court uniform. Since none existed, he designed and paid for one. When made up, it featured lavish quantities of gold embroidery around the coat's collar and cuffs, as well as a plumed tricorne hat.

Likewise, once he began to earn good money as a dealer in Old Master paintings, Lane never minded paying for beautiful items such as furniture. In Lindsey House on Cheyne Walk, a seventeenth-century property which became his home from 1909 onwards, he filled the principal rooms with valuable pieces by William Kent and Thomas Chippendale, as well as Grinling Gibbons carvings, Louis XV Aubusson carpets and a collection of Chinese and Japanese vases and figurines. And, of course, with a superb collection of Old Master paintings, his current choice displayed on an easel. For a while the first-floor drawing room held a grand piano, as Lane was fond of music, especially the romantics such as Chopin; typically, when the friend who had lent him the instrument asked for its return, he would not spend money on a replacement. The same parsimoniousness could be found in his own quarters where, in contrast to the luxury downstairs, his bedroom contained a plain white-painted bed and walls hung with old prints.

Meanwhile the garden to the rear of Lindsey House was designed for him by a close friend, the architect Edwin Lutyens, and the result described in the October 1912 edition of *Country Life* as showing 'a refined classical flavour without being stiff'. Lane loved plants and inside the house large arrangements of fresh flowers were forever to be seen in the reception rooms because, as Lady Gregory remarked, as far as her nephew was concerned 'flowers were a necessity, a part of the beauty of life; they must not only be fresh, but of the right colour for the harmony of the room'. This interest in interior decor extended beyond his own home. When, for example, Ellen Duncan assumed responsibility for Dublin's Municipal Gallery in October 1914, he wrote to her, 'I hope you will fill the vases with greens or flowers, it makes the Gallery look cared for'. Nor could he resist the opportunity to advise his friends whether they asked for him to do so or not. Fortunately some were happy to take direction. In her memoir, *Seventy Years Young*, Daisy, Countess of Fingall describes how at her request Lane devised a scheme for the refurbishment of Killeen Castle, County Meath. This involved painting the walls of the principal drawing room the colour of pale stone and having James Hicks, Dublin's best-known cabinet maker of the period, fill an alcove with light shelves on which a collection of *famille rose* and *famille verte* china could be displayed. As Lane then

Philip Wilson Steer
Lindsey House, Chelsea
1911
Oil on canvas, 74.9 x 57.2 cm
Purchased 1977

informed her, 'Anything beautiful will go together – particularly anything Chinese'. Lady Fingall wrote that he 'was indefatigable. He would arrange a room a dozen times and rearrange it before he was satisfied'. Entering a room, he had been known not merely to rearrange the ornaments on the chimneypiece but even to take down the curtains if these failed to please him. He even went so far as to tell one London hostess that her drawing room was 'like a bazaar'. No wonder Thomas Bodkin would remember Lane as being 'amazingly fastidious', to the point that his notepaper and envelopes were chosen because their shade of azure blue harmonised perfectly with the pink of the penny stamp; 'Except in an emergency, he would never degrade it with two green halfpenny stamps'. He also had a taste for gems; the sale of his effects after Lane's death included twenty-four lots of jewellery including a rose diamond hair ornament said to have belonged to the French queen Marie Antoinette.

Many of these pieces were bought after he had enjoyed success at the tables in Monte Carlo's casino. Lane liked to travel to the south of France every spring where, as was to be expected, he would stay at an inexpensive hotel and dine in cheap restaurants. Then, rather unexpectedly, he ventured to risk large sums in gambling. Bodkin believed his friend

Henri Fantin-Latour *Blush Roses*
c. 1860–1900
Oil on canvas, 44 x 36 cm
Presented by Lady Ardilaun, 1905

would annually 'lose several thousand pounds in a few weeks' play', and remembered that once he had become temporarily stranded in France when his money had run out and his banker refused to send any more. But Lane could sometimes win at the tables too, because Lady Gregory saw a notebook kept by her nephew in which he recorded the results of his gambling habit: 'Won £540. Bought diamond and pearl necklet £280'. On another occasion he wrote, 'Lost in evening all capital, £400. Bought three pearl strings and olivine ring for £233'. A friend who once met Lane in Paris remembered him returning from Monte Carlo with no money but a travelling bag full of loose pearls.

This fondness for gambling might appear out of character in a man who was frequently so thrifty, but Lane's whole career was built on an element of risk, taking a chance on pictures that might or might not prove to be a good investment. There was a streak of wildness in his persona that displayed itself in his reckless horse riding and later, when he bought a car, in having his chauffeur drive at the fastest speed possible. His febrile spirit meant he could never settle or even sit still for long. Outside of art he developed few interests and certainly nothing else managed to engage him with the same intensity. Books, for example, could not distract him and almost the only ones he possessed were monographs on Old Masters. 'Nothing but press cuttings', was how he summarised his reading habits to Joseph Solomon. Books required him to be sedentary and his feeble education had not encouraged any great fondness for them; he could always read a picture faster than a book. And alternative, more active, distractions could be found to absorb his time: the arrangement of furniture – his own or that of other people – and of flowers; the search for an appropriate gift to present to a friend; the organisation of social engagements, particularly afternoon tea parties, which were his preferred form of entertaining.

It is the apparent incongruities in Lane's character that give his life a particular interest. On the one hand, he was devoted to Ireland but never lived in the country (when in Dublin, he stayed in the United Serviceman's Club on St Stephen's Green). He was simultaneously parsimonious and extravagant, shy but sociable, highly knowledgeable about art yet unable to articulate that knowledge. His early death in 1915 means he missed enjoying success in the aftermath of the First World War experienced by other dealers like Joseph Duveen. Even in his short life, however, and despite beginning with many disadvantages, he accomplished an enormous amount and left Ireland a permanent legacy.

William Orpen *Hugh Lane Reading*
c. 1904
Pencil on paper, 22.9 x 17.7cm
Purchased, 1995

The Picture Dealer in Dublin: Hugh Lane's Municipal Gallery of Modern Art

MORNA O'NEILL

According to Hugh Lane, the Municipal Art Gallery presented an ideal focus for the art-loving dealer. As he explained, 'I never sell a picture until I am driven to it. And if I sell to some millionaire it is lost. I don't see it again, it may not give any very great pleasure to him and it is lost to everyone else. But if I give a picture to a gallery, that is really good business. It is as much mine as ever, I still possess it. I can see it when I like and everyone else can see it too, so that's no waste in the matter.'[1] In this remarkable explanation of his business philosophy, Lane expresses disdain for his clients and conflates philanthropy with the market imperative. This essay will discuss the way in which Lane positioned himself in the art market as a gentleman dealer and the way in which this professional identity informed the creation of the Municipal Gallery of Modern Art in Dublin, especially in regard to decoration. Here I mean both the ornamentation of the space, as in interior decoration, and an approach to painting that Edwardian critics described as 'decorative'. As I will discuss, the Dublin gallery, like Lane's success as a dealer, relied upon the values that underpinned the international art market: the individual vision and discernment of the connoisseur. Yet these same qualities prompted others to contest his role as cultural interpreter, and Lane found it difficult to sustain his identity as both 'dealer' and 'philanthropist'.

Hugh Lane, picture dealer

When Hugh Lane died in 1915, after German torpedoes sank the *Lusitania*, obituaries praised his selfless devotion to art and his atypical business practices in equal measure. The artist Henry Tonks, writing in *The Burlington Magazine*, described Lane as 'a picture dealer', but 'never in romance or real life has there been such a dealer before. If he had ambitions, it would be very difficult to say what they were; at least they were not those of a dealer'.[2] The critic D. S. MacColl noted in 1909 that Lane was 'a sort of dealer', while to the historian and collector Michael Sadler, Lane seemed 'an adventurous buyer of works of art' with 'an extraordinary intuition for what is good'.[3] Lane carefully constructed the professional identity of gentleman dealer suggested by these comments.

By 1909, Lane had been in business for more than fifteen years.[4] He began in the professional art dealer trade in 1893 with an apprenticeship at Martin Colnaghi's Marlborough Gallery, a position obtained through an introduction from Lady Gregory. Lane did not stay long, and he began to buy and sell as an independent agent in 1895. The following year, he joined the dealer E. Trevelyan Turner, manager of the Carlton Gallery, in a business venture: Turner would provide gallery space for the display of works acquired by Lane for a percentage of the sale price, and he would engage Lane as a 'finder' or 'buyer' of Old Master paintings. This arrangement also soured quickly, and Lane established his own rooms in Pall Mall in 1898, first on Pall Mall Place, and then later 47 Duke Street, and, finally, 93 Jermyn Street. Although his premises were at the heart of the London art dealer trade, Lane was eager to distance himself from 'the trade'.[5] By 1906, he was also sharing space with the artist William Orpen in South Bolton Gardens, storing and displaying works adjacent to the artist's studio.[6] He conducted his business along 'gentlemanly' lines, forgoing written contracts in favour of verbal agreements and, eventually, relocating his pictures to his home.

Lane moved his business into his home in 1909, when he acquired Lindsey House, part of a former seventeenth-century mansion at 100 Cheyne Walk in Chelsea. The move from the commercial West End to the more bohemian Chelsea further removed Lane's business from the usual trade. According to his friend and biographer Thomas Bodkin, Lane was an inveterate decorator, and Lindsey House became his showpiece.[7] While it was not unusual for dealers such as Paul Durand-Ruel and Duveen Brothers to set up apartments or devise mock domestic situations in which to invite clients to view works, it was unusual for the dealer himself to live on those premises as his home.[8] Lane settled at Lindsey House, and he commissioned decorative paintings from Augustus John for the front hallway (these were never fully realised, much to Lane's dismay), while the rest of the house displayed his taste for the seventeenth and eighteenth centuries: carvings by Grinling Gibbons above the mantelpiece, a prized cabinet designed by William Kent for Burlington House, and Jacobean oak panelling. These provided a backdrop for his collection of Chinese and Japanese ceramics as well as the paintings in his holdings. According to his friend, the architect

J. M. Solomon, Lindsey House evoked a range of artistic references: the bay window overlooked the Thames in a way that suggested 'Whistler's nocturnes' while the light in the room recalled the art of Rembrandt and Goya; Lane himself looked like an El Greco.[9] He courted potential clients by inviting them to tea, spilling out into the back garden designed by Edwin Lutyens; the dealer knew that such events were 'good for trade'.[10]

The movement of his business practice into his home in Chelsea contributed to Lane's identity as a 'gentleman dealer', one who 'formed a collection to please his own taste'.[11] This role seems to be Lane's own invention, although there are models for this type of behaviour among eighteenth-century antiquarians and connoisseurs. This rationale explains his habit of buying from and selling to other dealers, as 'each new item was paid for from the proceeds of the sale of something rejected to make way for it'.[12] The quality and coherence of his collection was the primary concern: Lane was a scrupulous curator of his collection. Lane's role as gentleman dealer, however, led his contemporary Joseph Duveen to dismiss him as an 'amateur'.[13] The gentlemanly domesticity of Lane's practice distinguishes him from competitors. Duveen, for example, drew upon a range of museum professionals and 'experts' such as Bernard Berenson, Wilhelm von Bode, and Robert Langton Douglas to authenticate works, often for a percentage of the profit.[14] Lane, in contrast, styled himself as an aesthete, and he used this reputation as a marketing tool that subverted the regularised commission structures and contracts. While Duveen stage-managed the firm's outposts and sold paintings alongside tapestry, furniture, ceramics and enamels, Lane's clients would, quite literally, buy the works of art from off the walls of his home.[15] The grandeur of Lindsey House performed a kind of alchemy: each work became a prized part of a gentleman's collection.

Lane's lack of academic training, as well as his lack of interest in the developing field of academic connoisseurship, meant that his judgments often remained based on his 'sixth sense': his eye for art.[16] Auctions proved to be a profitable source of pictures: he often purchased misattributed works or those in poor condition to clean (he sometimes did this work himself) and sell at a higher price.[17] Martin Colnaghi advised Lane that the most important training for a dealer was the viewing of as many works of art as possible in person; with this in mind, Lane toured country houses in Ireland throughout 1903. Lane's family background gave him access to aristocratic collections in Ireland, and it put him in a position to negotiate sales for impoverished Irish aristocrats.

Many of Lane's sales were enabled by two inter-related factors: the influx of paintings from British private collections onto the marketplace and Lane's background in the Irish 'Ascendancy'.[18] In the period between the 1880s and the 1930s, historian David Cannadine argues, the supply of aristocratic art collections and the demand of wealthy American collectors fuelled the art market.[19] The novelist George Moore recalls that one prominent Irish collector insisted on describing Lane as 'a London picture-dealer' and suspected that he 'had come to Ireland to see what he could pick up'.[20] A number of Irish families sought Lane's advice on selling works from their collections.[21]

With such sales, Lane became a purveyor of aristocratic provenance and, accordingly, contemporary accounts of his sales blur the boundaries between dealer and gentleman collector; a notice of the sensational sale of Titian's *Portrait of Philip II* (c. 1550; Cincinnati Museum of Art) by Mrs Thomas J. Emery in Cincinnati makes it sound as if Lane were not a businessman whose business was the sale of works of art: Mrs. Emery's friend Mary Morgan Newport visited Lane's home in London and noticed the Titian; 'I asked Sir Hugh if the painting could be bought. He replied in the affirmative'. The article describes the dealer as 'a noted English art connoisseur'.[22] Furthermore, a knighthood in 1909 from Edward VII in recognition of Lane's 'services to art' enhanced his status as a gentleman.[23]

Although their means and methods may have differed, Lane, Duveen and other dealers attempted to 'align' themselves with their customers as collectors and philanthropists.[24] According to Lane's biographers, the James Staats Forbes collection first piqued Lane's interest in French art, and he focused his own collecting on Impressionist art. [25] The Irish painter William Orpen had introduced Lane to the work of Édouard Manet and the Impressionists during a single day's visit to Paris in 1904. Lane described the dynamic between his roles as dealer and collector as 'selling pictures by old painters to buy pictures by living painters',[26] even though he rejected an invitation from the dealer Félix Fénéon to consider more recent work by Cézanne, Van Gogh and Matisse during one visit to Paris.[27] He relied upon the dealer Paul Durand-Ruel for most of his purchases, including his first acquisition: the larger version of Pierre Puvis de Chavannes's *Beheading of John the Baptist* (c. 1869; National Gallery, London).

According to art historian Philip McEvansoneya, Lane's subsequent collecting in this area often put him in competition with wealthier buyers, including the American collectors Louisine Havemeyer and Dr Albert C. Barnes.[28] However, many works remained beyond Lane's budget, especially since he was also adding to his dealer's holdings during trips to Paris. For example, during one visit to the city, he purchased a painting by Edgar Degas from the Henri Rouart collection

Edgar Degas *Beach Scene*
c. 1868-77
Oil essence on paper, mounted on canvas, 47 x 82.6cm
Sir Hugh Lane Bequest, 1917
The National Gallery, London

at a much publicised multi-day sale, as well as works by El Greco, Anthony Van Dyck and Thomas Gainsborough. Lane's subsequent purchases expanded his personal collection of French Impressionist pictures: in 1907, he acquired Pierre-Auguste Renoir's *The Umbrellas* (1881-86; National Gallery, London), among others, and he later purchased another group of Impressionist pictures in 1912.[29] For the most part, Lane's personal collection was not hung in his home; those works purchased before he announced his Dublin gallery were often placed on long-term loan with friends. William Orpen, for example, kept Manet's *Portrait of Eva Gonzalès* (1870; National Gallery, London) in his studio. Art acquired after the gallery opened was sent directly to Dublin. By locating his pictures for sale in his home, and then establishing a museum in Dublin for his personal collection, Lane effectively confused the categories of dealer, collector and philanthropist.

Lane first suggested a gallery of modern art in Dublin in 1905, and it opened to the public in temporary premises in January of 1908, displaying 280 works of art. The French Impressionist and other pictures that are now known as the 'conditional gift' of 39 paintings to be given to the city once they established a permanent home for the collection are the best known, but his collection also included British art, Irish art and portraits that Lane hoped would be the beginning of an Irish National Portrait Gallery. Most accounts of the gallery scheme focus on the disagreement between Lane and the Corporation of the City of Dublin over provisions for the collection.[30] Some critics accused Lane of seeking 'personal glorification' and a 'tremendous advertisement' for his business as an art dealer.[31] The rejection of his proposed scheme in 1913 by the Corporation led Lane to change his will and leave the pictures to the National Gallery in London. An un-witnessed codicil from 1915 transferred the pictures back to Dublin.

The contested legacy continues to this day, with the 'conditional gift', including the prized Impressionist pictures, shared by the National Gallery in London and what is now called Dublin City Gallery the Hugh Lane.[32] Art historian Fintan Cullen has suggested that Lane's gallery courted controversy because he envisioned an Irish identity beyond the boundaries of the British Empire. Lane wanted his gift to promote a 'national school' of Irish art, but his choice of modern French art moves beyond parochial notions of Irish identity and Irish art. Thus, according to Cullen, Lane posited a cosmopolitan, European identity.[33] I would suggest, however, that in his public comments and publications, as well as his organisation of exhibitions, Lane presented his gift as complementary to Irish identity. With his proposed gift of modern art to Dublin, Lane created an Irish identity for his French pictures by presenting them as part of a decorative tradition that included Celtic art.

Decoration in Dublin

Lane's interest in Irish art coincided with his introduction to the Celtic Revival circle of his aunt Augusta Gregory, and he organised a successful exhibition to aid the Royal Hibernian Academy in Dublin in 1902. He tried, unsuccessfully, to exhibit a collection of Irish art at the World's Fair in St Louis in 1904.[34] He showed those pictures at the Guildhall in London that same year. In a prefatory notice to the catalogue, Lane praises the artistic production of the Irish 'of early times', especially what he calls the 'perfect forms' of twelfth-century decorative practices.[35] He praises the decorative 'Irish race instinct' in literature, and suggests that 'it can hardly be absent in the sister art'.[36] This 'racial' view of Irish art was apparent to many critics who visited the exhibition, since 'the art they saw there was not Irish, but all those who produced it had Irish blood in their veins'.[37] He goes on to suggest that a gallery of modern art in Dublin would lead to the development of 'a distinct school of painting in Ireland'.[38]

Lane was not unique in his appreciation of the 'race instinct' in Irish art. This view can be traced back to rise of ethnography in the 1850s, and George Stocking pointed out the 'close articulation, both experiential and otherwise, between the domestic and colonial spheres of otherness' in his important *Victorian Anthropology*.[39] Within a Celtic context, Matthew Arnold's 1867 text 'On the Study of Celtic Literature' was perhaps the best-known Victorian exposition of this topic.[40] Arnold hoped to reconcile the 'Celtic' identity of the British people with the 'Teutonic' (and 'Norman'). By 1900, 'every educated Britain knew in outline the "racial" history of the British nation'.[41] Popular texts such as John Beddoe's *Races of Britain* from 1885 popularised this history even as it transformed mid-Victorian ethnocentrism into racism.

The novelist and evolutionist Grant Allen, in an essay from 1891, however, suggested the radical value of 'the Celt'. Allen applied Arnold's notion of the 'Celtic Genius' to the visual arts, in particular the painting *The Rose Bower* from *The Briar Rose Series* (1870-90, Faringdon Collection, Buscot Park, Oxfordshire), by the nominally Celtic Edward Burne-Jones. Allen believed in 'the Celtic wave of influence' that would overtake the 'Teuton' in English identity. These categories were probably influenced by the French art critic Ernest Chesneau, who first opposed the abstract nature of 'Latin art' to the realist impulse of 'Saxon art' in 1868.[42] Allen fuses these terms with his own socialist politics. Thus Burne-Jones's exemplary 'Celtic product' champions intricate fretwork pattern, overall design of a composition, and poetical, symbolic subject matter, in opposition to realistic, fact-based painting engendered by the industrialism and materialism of contemporary English life.[43] Allen summarises this Celtic artistic instinct as 'decorative', a tradition superior to and distinct from what he calls the 'imitative' and 'Teutonic' artistic impulse nurtured in England by the Anglo-Saxons.[44] For Allen, the Teutonic desire for 'technical mastery' too easily approaches the industrial imperatives of the late Victorian era.

The Celt in Britain 'like Mr Burne-Jones's enchanted princess, has lain silent for ages in an enforced long sleep' but it has returned with a vengeance, 'bringing [. . .] the Celtic characteristics into the very thick and forefront of the actual fray in England' which will lead to an eventual 'Celtic upheaval'.[45] Thus the 'Celtic temperament' has the potential to transform not only British art, but also British culture and British politics through socialism and Home Rule agitation. If, as contemporary

Black and white photograph
of the interior of the Municipal
Gallery of Modern Art, Clonmell
House, Harcourt Street, Dublin

'Dublin Municipal Art Gallery' in
Irish Independent, January 1908

authors suggested, the decorative art of a people reflected their character, then the Celt is an aesthete who values beauty above all. As Allen concludes, 'To the Celtic type of artist, the picture itself, as a lovely and glorious thing, is the end and aim of all'.[46] Given Lane's reputation as an aesthete, it would not be surprising if he found Allen's ideas appealing.

Lane, it seems, invested in this notion of Celtic decoration: in fact, he acquired Burne-Jones's *The Sleeping Princess* from the first *Briar Rose Series* (c. 1872-74, Dublin City Gallery The Hugh Lane) at an unknown date, and he made it the centrepiece of the British room in his Dublin gallery. Lane may not have offered interior decoration as part of his business, but he oversaw the adornment of each room of the gallery, including eighteenth-century furniture, ornamental ceramics and floral arrangements.[47] This decorative impulse further confused domestic space and gallery space, especially since the gallery occupied a Georgian townhouse in Harcourt Street. Lady Gregory recalls that Lane gave her and other ladies flowers at the opening and directed them to pose in certain corners of the galleries to add to the 'decorative effect' of the pictures.[48] The 'decorative' display of his galleries hearkened back to a 'gentlemanly' form of display popular in the seventeenth and eighteenth centuries that, according to Carol Duncan, 'subordinated individual works to larger decorative schemes, often surrounding them with luxurious furnishings and ornaments'.[49] He also devised a scheme to decorate his gallery with mural painting depicting important events from Irish craft, folklore and history.[50]

In Dublin at least, modern art merged with Celtic ornamentation: according to one (exasperated) Irish critic of Lane's gallery, 'we hear so much nowadays of the desirability of a school of distinctive Irish art. The man who draws intricate designs of interlaced ornament is looked on as an evangelist'.[51] Lane's exhibition efforts were often connected with Arts and Crafts activities as vernacular expressions of decorative art thought to embody 'Celticness'.[52] Dermot Robert Wyndham Bourke, the seventh Earl of Mayo, the honorary president of the Arts and Crafts Society in Ireland, spoke at the opening of Lane's 1905 exhibition and explicitly connected the dealer's efforts with those of the Arts and Crafts group.[53] Invitation cards to the opening of the gallery in 1908 were printed in Gaelic and English, as were labels and the catalogue.[54] Furthermore, Stephen Gwynn of the Gaelic League spoke at this event and declared Lane's project 'sympathetic' to the goals of the nationalist League.[55] Irish nationalists reclaimed the ethnographic notion of 'the decorative Celt', and both the 'Irish Ireland' brand of nationalism and the Celtic Revival promoted the innate artistry of the Irish people, as evident in the Broighter Hoard of Celtic gold discovered in 1896 and the celebrated Book of Kells.

Decoration thus provided a 'Celtic' context for the prized Impressionist pictures. Scholarly focus on the perceived modernity of the 'modern' pictures in Lane's collection, and their subsequent place in a teleological history of modern art, has overlooked the way in which decoration allowed Renoir's *Les Parapluies*, for example, to take its place alongside Edward Burne-Jones's *Briar Rose* as decorative. The term was a critical lynchpin in the late nineteenth century, deployed in numerous contexts to describe a diverse array of artistic production.[56] Meaning shifted depending on its context, but in discussions of both Renoir and Burne-Jones, it was used to denote an emphasis on colour and patterning of the painted surface as well as attention to the overall 'design' of the composition.[57] A number of artists in the Lane Collection were considered 'decorative' in outlook: Renoir and Monet, as well as Puvis de Chavannes, Giovanni Segnatini and Auguste Rodin, to name a few.[58] Despite a later modernist denial of decoration, scholars have argued that the decorative

Edward Burne-Jones *The Sleeping Princess*
c. 1872-74
Oil on canvas, 126 x 237 cm
Lane Bequest, 1913

can be found in the very patterns, vivid coloration and flowing lines that motivated the art of pure form.[59] I would argue that Lane gravitated to Impressionism as a marketable form of modernism that could be legitimised historically in Ireland through decoration.[60]

The ethnographic link between an Irish state, however ancient or imaginary, and a decorative Celtic art became a part of nationalist rhetoric in Ireland.[61] Lady Gregory argued for Lane's gallery scheme as a nationalist project in an editorial published in Gaelic in the Gaelic League weekly paper *An Claidheamh Soluis*.[62] The League and the paper became known as the mouthpiece of 'Irish Ireland', a term popularised in the 1890s.[63] Yet the final Corporation vote on the gallery divided Nationalist members.[64] Members withdrew their support from Lane, exasperated by what they saw as his desire for a monument to himself.[65]

A municipal art gallery takes art out of circulation as private property and transforms it into public good. Some critics portrayed the exhibition of works of art in public galleries as a form of 'emancipation' – a phraseology that echoes Lane's own comments on the 'loss' of works of art that are sold to millionaires. Yet Lane faced criticism in his role as 'arbiter' of local, national and imperial taste. How could he presume to collect for museum visitors in Dublin? According to historian Jordanna Bailkin, the first decade of the twentieth century witnessed a crisis in the 'material culture of Liberalism',[66] a growing suspicion of the public good posited by municipal museums, art education, and town planning. The fact that 'national' and 'imperial' culture rested in the hands of a few exacerbated this debate. Furthermore, modern aesthetic theory no longer viewed art as an instrumental social good.[67] As Carol Duncan has discussed, the museum in the early twentieth century shifted from the Enlightenment ideal of a place to 'enlighten and improve its visitors morally, socially, and politically' to the twentieth-century ideal of 'the aesthetic museum'.[68] Lane attempted to fuse these two elements, investing moral, social, and political purpose into the aesthetic of the decorative. Yet he found that he could not supplant the aristocratic owner of a work of art without being subject to the same critique. Lane could not sustain his identity as both 'dealer' and 'philanthropist', someone who, in his own words, 'never sells a picture' until he is 'driven to it'.[69]

An expanded version of this text was previously published in Anne Helmreich and Pamela Fletcher (eds.), *The Rise of the Modern Art Market in London, 1850-1939* (Manchester, 2011).

ENDNOTES

1   Lane, as quoted in James White, 'Sir Hugh Lane as a Collector', *Apollo*, 94, no. 144 (February 1974), 116.

2   Henry Tonks, 'Sir Hugh Lane', *Burlington Magazine*, 27, no.147 (June 1915), 128.

3   Typescript in Tate Archive, TD 28 October 1909, visit with D. S. MacColl to Augustus John and P. W. Steer, 8221.5.4. My thanks to Anne Helmreich for bringing this source to my attention.

4   For Lane's biography, see Robert O'Byrne, *Hugh Lane 1875-1915* (Dublin, 2000).

5   Lane's gallery at 93 Jermyn Street does not appear in *The Post Office London Directory for 1908* (London, 1908).

6   O'Byrne, *Hugh Lane*, 97.

7   Thomas Bodkin, *Hugh Lane and his Pictures* (Dublin, 1956), 70.

8   Martha Ward, 'Impressionist Installations and Private Exhibitions', *Art Bulletin*, 73 (December 1990), 599-622.

9   J.M. Solomon, 'Sir Hugh Lane: A Memoir', *Country Life in South Africa*, 1, no. 3 (June 1915), 11.

10 Bodkin, *Hugh Lane*, 70.

11 *Ibid.*, p. 3. The phrase is Bodkin's.

12 Bodkin, *Hugh Lane*, 3.

13 As quoted in O'Byrne, *Hugh Lane*, 93.

14 See Ernest Samuels, *Bernard Berenson: The Making of a Connoisseur* (Cambridge, Mass, 1979) 192-3, and John Simpson, *The Artful Partners: The Secret Partnership between Bernard Berenson and Joseph Duveen* (London, 1988) 87.

15 As described by Meryle Secrest, *Duveen: A Life in Art* (Chicago, 2005), 51. See also Colin B. Bailey, *Building the Frick Collection* (New York, 2006), 59-60.

16 Lady Gregory, *Hugh Lane's Life and Achievement, with Some Account of the Dublin Galleries* (London, 1921), 27.

17 As noted in O'Byrne, *Hugh Lane*, 23.

18 See Roy Foster, 'A Family Affair: Lane, Gregory, Yeats and Educating the Nation' in Barbara Dawson et al (eds.), *Hugh Lane. Founder of a Gallery of Modern Art for Ireland* (London, 2008), 29-36.

19 David Cannadine, *The Decline and Fall of the British Aristocracy* (New Haven, 2005), 113.

20 George Moore, *Hail and Farewell* (Gerrards Cross, 1985), vol. 2, 259.

21 Peter Mandler referred to this practice as 'maximizing the assets' of landholders. See Peter Mandler, *The Fall and Rise of the Stately Home* (London, 1997), 119.

22 'Mrs. Emery Buys a $400,000 Titian', *New York Times* (20 December, 1913), 1.

23 Gregory, *Hugh Lane's Life and Achievement*, p. 158, as quoted in O'Byrne, *Hugh Lane*, 117.

24 See, for example, Michelle Lapine, 'Mixing Business with Pleasure: Asher Wertheimer as Art Dealer and Patron' in *John Singer Sargent: Portraits of the Wertheimer Family* , exhib. cat. (New York, 1999), 46.

25 See Edward Morris, *French Art in Nineteenth-Century Britain* (New Haven and London, 2005), 242-3.

26 *Ibid.*, 164.

27 Un-catalogued Hugh Lane letters, National Library of Ireland, Acc. 5073.

28 Philip McEvansoneya, 'Lane's Choices: Degas, Monet, Pissarro and Puvis de Chavannes' in Barbara Dawson et al (eds.), *Hugh Lane. Founder of a Gallery of Modern Art for Ireland* (London, 2008), 37.

29 *Ibid.*, 40.

30 See Dawson, *Hugh Lane*, 13-33 and Neil Sharp, 'The wrong twigs for an eagle's nest? Architecture, Nationalism and Sir Hugh Lane's scheme for a Gallery of Modern Art in Dublin 1904-13 ' in M. Giebelhausen (ed.), *The Architecture of the Museum* (Manchester and New York, 2003), 32-53.

31 As noted in 'Dublin and Sir Hugh Lane', *Weekly Irish Times* (25 January 1913), 10.

32 Lucy McDiarmid, *The Irish Art of Controversy* (Dublin, 2005), 38-9.

33 Fintan Cullen, 'The Lane Bequest', *Field Day Review*, 4 (2008), 187-201.

34 See Nicola Gordon Bowe, *Art and the National Dream: The Search for Vernacular Expression in Turn-of-the-Century Design* (Dublin, 1993), 16.

35 Lane, *Irish Painters*, ix

36 *Ibid*, x

37 'Pictures and Picture Galleries', *Weekly Irish Times* (31 December 1904), 16. For the 'Irishness' of this art, see also P. G. Konody, 'About Art. New Municipal Gallery at Dublin', *The Observer* (26 January 1908), 10.

38 Lane, *Irish Painters*, x

39 George W. Stocking, *Victorian Anthropology* (New York, 1987), 234.

40 Arnold, *Celtic Literature*. These essays first appeared as 'On the Study of Celtic Literature' in the *Cornhill Magazine* in 1867.

41 James Urry, 'Englishmen, Celts, and Iberians' in George Stocking (ed.), *Functionalism Historicized* (Wisconsin, 1984), 83.

42 As discussed in Patricia Mainardi, *Art and Politics of the Second Empire* (New Haven and London: Yale University Press, 1990), p. 163.

43 G. Allen, 'The Celt in English Art', *The Fortnightly Review*, 55 (n.s. 49), 1 February 1891, 267.

44 *Ibid.*, 268.

45 *Ibid.*, 267.

46 *Ibid.*, 271.

47 For museum décor, see Giles Waterfield, *Palaces of Art: Art Galleries in Britain 1790-1990* (London, 1991), 49-65.

48 Gregory, *Hugh Lane's Life*, 49.

49 Carol Duncan, *Civilizing Rituals: Inside Public Art Museums* (London, 1995), 25.

50 O'Byrne, *Hugh Lane*, 171.

51 'Gallery of Modern Art in Dublin', *Cork Examiner*, 8 March 1907 in MS 35,827/6, Scrapbook compiled by Ruth Shine, 1885-1907, National Library of Ireland, Dublin.

52 See Nicola Gordon Bowe, 'The Search for Vernacular Expression' in Bert Denker (ed.), *Substance and Style* (Winterthur, 1996), 5-24 and Nicola Gordon Bowe, 'A Contextual Introduction to Romantic Nationalism' in Bowe, *Art and the National Dream*, 181-200.

53 In an article entitled 'The Art Movement in Dublin' from 18 April 1905, a correspondent for the *Dublin Express* relates that the Earl of Mayo connected Lane's efforts to the Arts and Crafts movement. MS 35,827/6, Scrapbook compiled by Ruth Shine, 1885-1907, NLI, Dublin.

54 Bodkin, *Hugh Lane*, 19.

55 Press clipping from the *Dublin Express*, MS 35,827/6, Scrapbook compiled by Ruth Shine, 1885-1907, NLI, Dublin.

56 For cogent summaries of this issue, see Mark Cheetham, *The Rhetoric of Purity* (Cambridge, 1991).

57 For Renoir, see Robert Herbert, *Nature's Workshop* (New Haven and London, 2000), 66. For Burne-Jones, see Caroline Arscott, *William Morris and Edward Burne-Jones: Interlacings* (New Haven, 2008), 203-24.

58 See, for example, Robert Herbert, 'The Decorative and Natural in Monet's Cathedrals' in J. Rewald and F. Weitzenhoffer (eds.) *Aspects of Monet* (New York, 1984); Steven Z. Levine, 'Claude Monet's Art', *Arts Magazine*, 51 (February 1977); J.L. Shaw, *Dream States* (New Haven, 2002).

59 As discussed by Jenny Anger, *Paul Klee* (New York, 2004), 2.

60 Robert Jensen, *Marketing Modernism in Fin-de-Siècle Europe* (Princeton, 1994), 3. See also D.W.Galenson and Robert Jensen, 'Careers and Canvases' (National Bureau of Economic Research Working Paper, no. 9123, 2002), accessed 23 March 2008.

61 See, for example, Paul Larmour, *The Arts and Crafts Movement in Ireland* (BelfasT, 1992), Jeanne Sheehy, *The Rediscovery of Ireland's Past* (London, 1980) and Theiding, 'Anxieties of Influence'.

62 Reprinted in Gregory, *Hugh Lane's Life*, 62-4.

63 F.S.L. Lyons, *Ireland Since the Famine*,(London, 1971), 320-1. See also Donal MacCartney, 'MacNeill and Irish-Ireland' in F.X. Martin et al (eds.), *The Scholar Revolutionary* (Shannon, 1967), 77.

64 See Joseph O'Brien, *"Dear Dirty Dublin": a City in Distress 1899-1916* (University of California Press, 1982), 56.

65 As quoted in McDiarmid, *Irish Art of Controversy*, 27.

66 Jordanna Bailkin, *The Culture of Property* (Chicago, 2004).

67 Janet Minihan, *The Nationalization of Culture* (New York, 1977), 167.

68 Duncan, *Civilizing Rituals*, 16.

69 Lane, as quoted in White, 'Hugh Lane', 116.

Black and white photograph of Daniel Egan and his wife Annie Egan, 'Our Egan Lineage', EG/011, Collection National Irish Visual Arts Library (NIVAL), NCAD, Dublin.

Hugh Lane and the Firm of Daniel Egan, Ormond Quay: The Recollections of Joseph Egan

JESSICA O'DONNELL

Located at 26 Lower Ormond Quay in Dublin, the firm of Daniel Egan specialised in 'high class' framing, carving, gilding and fine art packing as well as picture cleaning and furniture restoration. The firm had its origins in the early nineteenth century and the business's reputation grew with each succeeding generation. Under Daniel Egan (1865-1910), who had taken over from his father in 1886, the firm counted a number of high-ranking people among their distinguished clients. One such person was the wife of the Lord Lieutenant of Ireland, who wrote a testimonial praising the Daniel Egan firm for the work they had carried out at the vice-regal lodge in the Phoenix Park.

Daniel Egan worked closely with Hugh Lane and, following Lane's untimely death in 1915 and the succession of Daniel Egan's son Joseph (1894-1983) as head of the family business in 1918, the company continued to work with the Municipal Gallery of Modern Art. The National Irish Visual Arts Library (NIVAL) in NCAD now houses the Egan Gallery Collection. Here, Joseph Egan's hand-written recollections, which he titled 'Diary of My Art Activities', offer fascinating insights on Hugh Lane, the Municipal Gallery and the Dublin art scene from a little-known perspective. His vignettes reveal how much he looked up to Hugh Lane and how the influence of Lane's achievements inspired him in his own career.[1]

Joseph learned all aspects of the Egan business from a young age. He remembered that as a young boy in 1904 he would wander into his father's packing warehouses. The place, he recalled, was full of pictures and he was given the task of running crate screws through soap to make them easier to put in and take out. These crates, he remembered, were intended for Lane's exhibition of Irish art at the St Louis World's Fair, an enterprise that unfortunately never came to fruition.

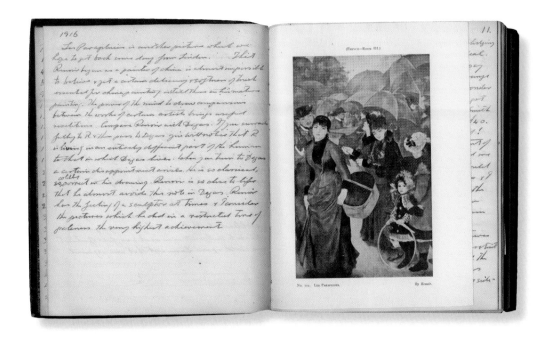

Joseph Egan, 'Diary of My Art Activities', EG/003, Collection
National Irish Visual Arts Library (NIVAL), NCAD, Dublin.

For a time Joseph attended night classes at the Metropolitan School
of Art where he found Margaret Clarke, the wife of the artist Harry
Clarke, to be a particularly inspirational teacher. However, the more
immediate pressures of the family business meant he had to abandon
his studies there. At the young age of only twenty-four he became head
of the Daniel Egan firm. Managing a business around the time of the
birth of the Irish State in the early 1920s was not easy. As Joseph wrote
in his diary: 'The conditions of business have changed. The Quays as a
business centre is destroyed since the Four Courts was blown up. Here
I stand in my shop day after day & no one comes…The whole
circumstances of business is changing rapidly as the political situation
changes. The business …requires cultured people to make it go at all'.[2]

In 1916, Joseph had had some success buying and selling art and
with the profits bought a Harley-Davidson motorcycle with a sidecar. It
was then, as he said himself, that he 'went deeper into politics'. While
not officially affiliated with the Nationalist movement, Joseph on his
motorcycle featured in a number of daring missions at the request of

the rebel leaders prior to and during the week of the Easter Rising in Dublin.[3] This innate daring and energy was echoed a number of years later, when in an attempt to improve his business situation, he moved the Daniel Egan firm to 38 St Stephen's Green in 1925. 'I must have startled the town', he wrote in his diary, reflecting the significance of the move. At St Stephen's Green, Joseph became something of an art entrepreneur. Here, he was an art dealer, organised exhibitions and established among other initiatives the Daniel Egan Salon; an Art Cabaret; the New Dublin Art Club and published the *Dublin Art Monthly* magazine while still retaining the Daniel Egan firm's name and traditional business of framing, picture restoration and art movement.

Joseph Egan's diary opens in 1915 with the dramatic line: 'Hugh Lane is dead. Art has suffered a blow in Dublin and the house of Egan too'. The loss to Ireland of the Lane Bequest paintings was also keenly felt and reproductions of these paintings are interspersed throughout his diary accompanied by reflections such as '*Les Parapluies* is another picture which we hope to get back some day from London'. Joseph wrote that every time he went to the Municipal Gallery he remembered the day in 1913 when the Daniel Egan firm took Lane's Continental pictures to the Mansion House where they were packed prior to being sent to London. As publisher of the *Dublin Art Monthly*, Joseph Egan took the opportunity in the magazine's very first issue in 1927 of highlighting how the Lane Bequest paintings' artistic and commercial value could be worth 'a million a year to Dublin in tourist traffic alone'. It was time, the opinion piece continued, that 'the trading community of Dublin aroused itself and took an active interest in this question, if necessary in financing a new demand to have justice done in the matter'. While eschewing the idea of entering into 'legal quibbles', the magazine stated that 'the attitude of Irish artists and art-lovers is simple – the pictures are ours by moral right, and we rely upon the moral generosity of English art lovers to have them restored to us'. [4]

Hugh Lane was adept at persuading artists and patrons to donate works to his proposed Gallery of Modern Art. In those early days, Joseph recalls, it was not always easy to foresee how Lane was to make Dublin distinguished by his visionary project. The generous support of Lane's activities spilled over to the commercial sphere when, according to Joseph Egan, Hugh Lane asked Daniel Egan to pay charges due on pictures as they arrived in Dublin. Joseph's aunt Annie recalled how Daniel Egan had to borrow money from her in order to do this but that he was a willing co-operator with Lane's plans. Joseph asks in his diary: 'could Lane have brought this Gallery into existence without my father

Black and white photograph of interior of Egan Studio, EG/006,
Collection National Irish Visual Arts Library (NIVAL), NCAD, Dublin.

and his willing collaboration?' According to him, Lane, who had little formal education but had amassed immense knowledge of pictures from direct experience, frequently asked Daniel Egan for his advice and clearly valued the opinion of this skilled craftsman. Daniel Egan worked readily for Lane, even though it was not clear who was to pay the bill. As Joseph recalls, Dublin Corporation was very divided about the Gallery. They eventually paid but, he says, 'I know only too well the long delay there was getting the money. My father died before it was paid'.[5] However, Daniel Egan's faith in Hugh Lane made good business sense. When Lane became Director of the National Gallery of Ireland in 1914, he did not forget the firm and Joseph remembers how they got more work there than ever they did before.

In his diary there are anecdotal details, perhaps remembered from his father, about Hugh Lane and the talented, but eccentric Italian

Black and white photograph of Antonio Mancini
and Ruth Shine, Harcourt Street, Dublin.

painter Antonio Mancini. Lane invited the artist, whom he greatly admired, to Dublin and a studio was set up at the top of the Municipal Gallery, then in Harcourt Street. There, Mancini painted portraits of Lane's sister Ruth Shine and his aunt Augusta, Lady Gregory, using a lawn tennis net for his famous *graticola*. This threaded grid, which was used by the artist to achieve the exact tone and proportions he wanted, was set up in front of the sitter at one end of the room with a second grid in front of the canvas at the other end. Joseph records how Mancini would dart between the two with his paintbrush pointed disconcertingly towards the subject like a pistol at a victim. As Mancini could not speak a word of English, Joseph wrote how Lane quickly commandeered an Italian named Anzani, who worked as a clerk for Daniel Egan, to act as interpreter while Mancini was in Dublin. According to Joseph, the clerk would recount amusing stories of

Interior view of the Municipal Gallery of Modern Art,
Clonmell House, 17 Harcourt Street, Dublin.

narrowly averted misunderstandings between Lane and the artist. Joseph Egan also records in his diary the legend of Hugh Lane, who hated waste of any sort, scraping some of the thick impasto paint off Mancini's canvases while the artist was out at lunch. As Lane was paying for all the artist's materials, he would then place the excess paint back on the artist's palette so that it could be re-used.

Joseph Egan came to know Hugh Lane personally when the Egan firm was engaged to hang pictures at the Municipal Gallery. As Daniel Egan's firm had earned praise for their interior decoration elsewhere, it is possible that they were also directed by Lane to assist with the physical arrangement of the antique furniture visible in early photographs of the interior of the Municipal Gallery.[6] Joseph also came to know Lane when he called to the Egan premises to see how frames were progressing. Lane's interest in frames is demonstrated, for example, by Manet's *Portrait of Eva Gonzalès*. Hugh Lane had bought the painting from the art dealer Paul Durand-Ruel and an illustration of *Eva Gonzalès* with the ornate frame it now has was included in a feature in the *Irish Independent* showing the interior of the Municipal Gallery when it first opened on 20 January 1908.[7] This contrasts with the less ornate frame visible in a photograph of the painting at the Grafton Galleries exhibition in London organised by Paul Durand-Ruel in 1905 just prior to Hugh Lane having acquired it.[8]

While exact details regarding frames are not recorded, Joseph says that he remembered well Lane's quiet way – how there was 'no fuss' and that 'it was a pleasure too'. He says that Lane was misunderstood, and that without any conceit he could take the best advice and act on it.

In 1933, when the Municipal Gallery moved to Charlemont House, Joseph Egan moved all the pictures, sculpture and furniture from Harcourt Street to the Gallery's new home. John J. Reynolds, then the Municipal Gallery's curator, also engaged Joseph Egan to arrange and hang the pictures in the new spaces. In tendering for the job, Joseph wrote, 'As I personally worked on the hanging of these pictures many years ago I am familiar with the responsibility and with my life-long acquaintance with the handling of valuable pictures I can guarantee the best service'. He recalls that his estimate was low and that not a single object was damaged.

Joseph also installed the Municipal Gallery's inaugural exhibition of sculpture and drawings by Rodin in 1933. As Rodin's *Age of Bronze* had graced the cover of the original Municipal Gallery catalogue in 1908, the choice of artist was especially apt. Joseph recalls how he also sent out invitations to the opening from his own register of art patrons, as he says Reynolds had none. Taking a great interest in the whole affair, he advised on the press coverage and emphasised the importance of having a good lecture to engage the public. In his diary he muses, 'The new Gallery has its defects but it is a wonderful thing to see it. I have been thinking of Sir Hugh Lane all the year'.

Moving the contents from Harcourt Street to Charlemont House brought back memories of Lane's achievements. In Joseph's opinion, 'Lane could not have lived and accomplished his task in this angular period'. He reflected that Hugh Lane had a democratic intuition through which the spirit of the ages worked, enabling him to achieve something wonderful in a short period of years. 'Goodness is giving', he writes. '…that is my definition of goodness; and Lane was full of giving,

Installation view of the Municipal Gallery of Modern Art,
Charlemont House (1933)

of goodness'. Echoing the words of the artist Augustus John, Joseph Egan wrote how Lane's generosity continued to enrich Ireland even after his death, both with the Lane Fund, (which benefits the National Gallery of Ireland) and the existence of the Municipal Gallery. It is fascinating to see in Joseph Egan's diary how Hugh Lane's vision at a pivotal moment in Irish history continues to resonate. For Joseph Egan there was little doubt that 'in a period of transition from the old Aristocratic regime to a dawning Democratic one, Lane appears and truly serves the future'.

ENDNOTES

1   I am very grateful to the staff of NIVAL at the National College of Art and Design (NCAD) for facilitating my access to the Egan Gallery Collection.

2   Joseph Egan, 'Diary of My Art Activities', EG/003, Egan Gallery Collection, NIVAL, NCAD.

3   Patrick Egan and Donal Egan, *Our Egan Lineage 1763-1993, A Compilation from Family Archives* (1997), 26, EG/011, Egan Gallery Collection, NIVAL, NCAD.

4   'Comment', *The Dublin Art Monthly*, October 1927, (vol. 1 no.1), 17. The magazine was published by Joseph Egan and the editor was George Edmund Lobo.

5   Daniel Egan died on 15 September 1910. His sister Annie Egan was the administrator of the business until Joseph Egan formally took it over in 1918.

6   This furniture remains part of Dublin City Gallery The Hugh Lane today.

7   *Irish Independent*, 21 January 1908.

8   A photograph of the interior of the Impressionist exhibition at the Grafton Galleries, London in 1905 is reproduced in S. Patry et al (eds.), *Inventing Impressionism: Paul Durand-Ruel and the Modern Art Market,* National Gallery, London (London, 2015), 231.

Simeon Solomon
The Bride from the Song of Solomon
1872
Pastel on panel, 39.5 x 16.5 cm
Lane Gift, 1912

The Works of Simeon Solomon in the Hugh Lane Gallery

CAROLYN CONROY

In March 1900, Augusta, Lady Gregory, recorded visiting Christie's auction house in London with her nephew Hugh Lane because there were 'Simeon Solomon's to be sold.'[1] At the time Lane was very disparaging of his aunt's enthusiasm for 'modern work' and in Lady Gregory's opinion, 'seemed puzzled, almost pitying' of her interest in Solomon.[2] Despite setting her heart on a 'lovely little thing of a musician,' Lady Gregory was outbid, and the 'beautiful' painting was sold to a higher bidder for the sum of fourteen pounds.[3] Lady Gregory suggested that at the time of this sale Lane had not yet 'made the rule he practised later and to the end of his life' of 'making money by selling old masters that he might spend it on living ones.'[4]

However, by 1904 Lane was well on the way to making the transition to collecting 'modern works', and on 2 July 1904 attended the sale of the art collection of recently deceased barrister Charles Alfred Swinburne. At the auction house of Christie, Manson and Woods in London, Lane bought four vibrant watercolours by Solomon titled: *The Bride from the Song of Solomon* (1872), and the *Bridegroom from the Song of Songs* (1873), *A Jewish King and his Page* (1873), and *Greeks Going to a Festival* (1873).[5] In the same year Lane also purchased Solomon's oil painting *The Finding of Moses* dated 1862 and the artist's pencil sketch from 1868 (dedicated to Oxford don Walter Pater), *The Bride, the Bridegroom and Friend of the Bridegroom*. All six of Solomon's works were subsequently gifted by Lane to the Municipal Gallery in 1912 and remain an important part of the Gallery's collection. This essay discusses four of these works, their provenance, context and homoerotic content, and their controversial maker Simeon Solomon – described by Oscar Wilde in 1877 as 'that strange genius.'[6]

It has only been in recent years, since a revival of interest in the work of the Pre-Raphaelites and the rise of LGBT and queer studies, that

Simeon Solomon *The Finding of Moses*
1862
Oil on canvas, 81.3 x 61 cm
Lane Gift, 1912

Simeon Solomon *The Bride, the Bridegroom and Friend of the Bridegroom*
1868
Pencil and conté on paper, 50.8 x 45 cm
Lane Gift, 1912.

a renewed interest in Solomon and his art has been generated. Solomon was born in 1840 in Bishopsgate Without in London's East End. He was the youngest of the eight surviving children of prosperous Jewish merchant Michael Solomon and his wife Catherine. Two of Solomon's siblings, older brother Abraham and sister Rebecca were already established and successful artists in their own right by the time that their younger brother became noticed. By the age of eighteen, Solomon had become something of an artistic prodigy, and had already met and befriended his hero, Pre-Raphaelite artist Dante Gabriel Rossetti, and was working at times in Rossetti's studio. This introduction into Rossetti's circle allowed Solomon the opportunity to fraternise with, and ultimately befriend the leading British artists, writers and poets of the day, including painters Edward Burne-Jones and John Everett Millais, and poet Algernon Swinburne to name a few. Early on Solomon's paintings reflected Jewish and old-testament themes and he was greatly influenced by Rossetti's Pre-Raphaelite style; however, these ideas were gradually overtaken by the Classical subjects preferred by his new friend Swinburne. Ultimately Swinburne's influence and encouragement would manifest itself in Solomon's choice of homoerotic and sado-masochistic imagery, and other ideas and themes that would become increasingly appealing to Solomon including sexual ambiguity and effeminacy.

Rossetti's brother William was one of the first to hail the 'real genius' and 'wonderful merit' of Solomon's paintings, and applaud the 'exhaustless fertility and quaintness of invention' of the artist's first Royal Academy exhibit in 1858, predicting for Solomon a future 'career of greatness.'[7] While William Makepeace Thackeray publicly lavished praise upon him Burne-Jones would ultimately describe Solomon as 'the greatest artist of us all.'[8] Solomon was not without his critics, however, and in 1871 would be fiercely ridiculed and scorned as a member of Rossetti's 'fleshly school' of artists and poets by critic Robert Buchanan for lending 'actual genius to worthless subjects' with his 'pretty pictures of morality.'[9] Solomon's reaction to this criticism was almost fatalistic. In a letter to Swinburne he appeared to be fully aware that his 'designs and pictures' were being 'looked upon with suspicion,' and he acknowledged, somewhat prophetically, that he would 'probably have to suffer still.'[10]

The suffering that Solomon predicted was soon to manifest itself, and a little under two years later, in February 1873, and at the height of his artistic fame, Solomon was arrested for attempted sodomy in a public urinal off Oxford Street with sixty-year-old stableman George Roberts. Both men were convicted of unlawfully committing 'the

Simeon Solomon
The Bridegroom from the Song of Songs
1873
Pastel on panel, 38 x 16 cm
Lane Gift, 1912

abominable crime of buggery.'[11] Roberts was subsequently sentenced to eighteen months hard labour in the House of Correction at Cold Bath Fields, while Solomon escaped a custodial sentence and was released to the care of his cousin Myer Salaman on a surety of £100, and the promise that he behaved himself. This promise was short lived, and almost a year later the artist was convicted of 'outrage to the public decency' in a Parisian public urinal with seventeen-year-old 'shop boy' Henri Lefranc.[12] The court sentenced Solomon to three months in a Paris jail, where it is likely he stayed until he returned to England in late 1874.

The impact of Solomon's initial arrest would be sudden and immediate. The artistic elite would instantly distance themselves from him, and his former friend Algernon Swinburne would proclaim him 'a thing unmentionable alike by men and women' and 'as equally abhorrent to either.'[13] With his patrons disappearing, commissions drying up, a reliance on alcohol becoming increasingly more evident and a continued refusal to 'reform', by early 1879 Solomon was destitute and requesting admission to the workhouse. He would subsequently die in the St Giles workhouse in 1905 some twenty-six years later.

Most histories would have you believe that there is little more to the story. That Solomon's withdrawal from respectable London society, his alcoholism and his apparent unwillingness to cooperate with any kind of rehabilitation, either physical or psychological, was a sign of his vulnerability, not of any kind of strength or determination. Indeed, the subsequent reaction to Solomon by writers was determined by comparisons made to the similar situation that was presented to the very different Oscar Wilde twenty years later. In essence Wilde's 'tragedy' became Solomon's.

The four Solomon watercolour paintings that Hugh Lane purchased in London from the posthumous art sale of Scottish-born barrister Charles Alfred Swinburne in 1904 (no relationship to Solomon's friend, poet Algernon Swinburne), are particularly important and relevant to an understanding of the artist's intentions in terms of his artwork and his sexuality. This is because they were commissioned and executed particularly during the key years surrounding Solomon's arrest in 1873. In addition, they offer an insight into the artist's use of a personal complex coded symbolism. The paintings also assist in undoing prior notions that Solomon was simply abandoned by his family and friends during the year of his arrest and instead they reveal an artist continuing to actively work on paintings which reflected his sexuality.

From an examination of the information contained on the backs of the paintings and by studying Charles Alfred Swinburne's catalogue of his collection, privately published in 1900, it can be ascertained that the barrister commissioned the paintings in 1872.[14]

According to the catalogue, Solomon was 'then a young man, a famous colourist, and a rising painter.'[15] C. A. Swinburne ordered the works for his large detached home at 32 Upper Hamilton Terrace in north-west London. He allowed Solomon to choose the subjects of the paintings, but asked him 'to show that watercolours could produce a beauty, a brilliancy, and intensity of colour equal to any oil painting.'[16] Solomon certainly appears to have achieved this, and C. A. Swinburne was very pleased with the result saying that he had 'nothing finer as regards colour' in his collection.[17]

The *Bride* and the *Bridegroom* were probably the first two paintings completed by Solomon for the Swinburne commission in 1872 and 1873.[18] Their theme reflects Solomon's lifelong obsession, reworking, and re-examination of imagery taken from the biblical book the *Song of Songs* or the *Song of Solomon* in the Old Testament, which he surreptitiously used to explore ideas of same-sex love in a private mythology and iconography which is often difficult to interpret. The Bride and the Bridegroom are the principle characters in the *Song of Songs*. In Solomon's painting, the Bridegroom is dressed as a pilgrim and is shown knocking on the door of the Bride's chamber requesting entry. As C. A. Swinburne notes in his catalogue, the pendant panels illustrate a scene from chapter 5 of the Song of Songs, verses 2, 5 and 6:

> I sleep, but my heart waketh: it is the voice of my beloved that knocketh
> saying, open to me, my sister, my Love, my dove, my undefiled:
> For my head is filled with dew, and my locks with the drops of the night.
> I arose up to open to my beloved; and my hands dropped with myrrh, and
> my fingers with sweet smelling myrrh, upon the handles of the lock.
> I opened to my beloved; but my beloved had withdrawn himself,
> and was gone.

The Bride in the companion painting is clothed in loose drapery with one small breast unconsciously revealed in an implied eroticism. The image is reminiscent of Rossetti's red-headed, thick-necked Pre-Raphaelite women not unlike the portrayal of his famous muse Fanny Cornforth from the 1860s, but Solomon's figure is different, it is androgynous – without sex - this Bride is meant to be neither male nor female. As Solomon explained to one of his earlier patrons, the Liverpool industrialist Frederick Leyland, of a similar work that he executed for Leyland representing the Bride and Bridegroom:

I mean the whole thing to represent Love in its very highest and most spiritual form, it is therefore sexless; I have mingled the sexes… the head although not that of a male is not female as you may see by the form of the jaw. Love in its highest form is above and beyond consideration of sex, which would at once limit and animalise it.[19]

Solomon's definition of the epitome of Love as sexless was imagined by the Victorian Aesthetes such as Solomon's close friends Walter Pater and Algernon Swinburne. According to Thais E. Morgan Pater and Swinburne celebrated the idea of androgynous beauty because it allowed for 'a reimagining of masculinity at the margins of conventional middle-class notions of manliness.'[20] This new interpretation of male beauty and male-male desire in the form of the androgynous figure was seen as preferable to the heterosexual norm and ultimately seen by Aesthetes as the cultural ideal. By the use of androgynous imagery, Solomon transposes the erotic heterosexual poetry of the *Song of Songs* and makes it his own very personal concept of same-sex love.

The Bride and the Bridegroom also make a significant appearance in Solomon's allegorical prose poem *A Vision of Love Revealed in Sleep*, privately published in 1871.[21] The poem reflects the artist's personal iconography which describes a narrator and his soul journeying through an unidentified, but Classically-inspired landscape whilst in a dream state where they experience visions of various forms and conditions including Pleasure, Passion, Sleep and Death, in a quest for the ultimate 'True' and 'Divine Love' or Solomon's embodiment of male-male desire. Many of Solomon's recurring symbolic motifs and images appear in both this poem and his artworks from the same and earlier periods. For example, the figure in the painting of the *Bridegroom* is reminiscent of the description of the narrator in the allegory who is 'clad as a traveller' holding a staff.[22] Like the narrator in the poem, the Bridegroom is also a pilgrim seeking some kind of enlightenment or education and an indication of this is the glass ball or crystal globe attached to a cloth sash around his waist. The use of the globe motif is repeated in many of Solomon's works and is an important symbol in his personal iconography of male-male love. It seems likely to refer back to one of the assertions in the poem that 'knowledge' may be sought or understanding made clearer via visions seen 'as in a glass' and ultimately that 'yearning' or 'great desire' will be fulfilled by them.[23] This idea may have allusions to the biblical phrase 'through a glass darkly' from Corinthians 13.12, in which an obscure or imperfect vision of reality will ultimately be made clearer in a 'glass' or mirrored surface, or in Solomon's case, a crystal

Simeon Solomon
A Jewish King and his Page
1873
Watercolour and gouache
on paper, 23 x 23 cm
Lane Gift, 1912

ball. Indeed, Solomon's visions in the glass globe are difficult to behold as illustrated in the poem by the 'the lips' of Morpheus (who guides the sleeper's dreams), which 'trembled with the weight of the myriads of visions he called forth'.[24]

In addition to the globe motif, two of Solomon's other recurring images are the budding staff and flowering myrtle plant. In his right hand the Bridegroom holds a staff with a branch of myrtle either wrapped around it or growing out of its top. In his letter to Leyland, Solomon describes this kind of image as 'the dead stick, blossoming into myrtle flowers, like Aaron's rod that budded' symbolising that which was 'thought dead is ever freshly blooming.'[25] This is perhaps a reference in the poem to the restoration of Solomon's allegorical personification of Love, characterised as a winged male youth, who in the early visions is shown bound, bloodied and beaten almost to death; but by the end is ultimately transformed back to life into the 'Very Love' or Solomon's 'Divine type of Absolute Beauty.'

The myrtle plant was associated with everlasting love and conjugal fidelity during the Renaissance period and was sacred to Venus/ Aphrodite, the Classical goddess of love, pleasure, beauty and procreation. In this way, Solomon uses myrtle in both a secular and sacred context throughout his work to signify and perhaps even embody his concept of the 'Very Love.' Indeed, at the beginning of

Simeon Solomon *King Solomon*
1872 or 74
Egg tempera (?) with touches of varnish
on paper mounted to board, 39.5 x 21.5 cm
Gift of William B. O'Neal
The National Gallery of Art, Washington, D.C

Solomon's dream quest, Love is 'dethroned and captive' with his wings 'broken and torn' while the myrtle 'upon his brow', now clearly a mirror of Love's suffering, is described as 'withered and falling'.[26] The myrtle plant was seemingly also important to other Aesthetes in Solomon's circle, and a direct association with the myrtle plant and Solomon is made in a book of poetry published in 1883 and titled *Myrtle, Rue and Cypress*.[27] The author was Solomon's future patron and close friend, the outrageous and flamboyant Aesthete and friend of Oscar Wilde, Count Eric Stanislaus Stenbock. On the dedication page of the book of poetry Stenbock revealed his passion for Solomon by dedicating the 'myrtle thereof' to the artist.[28]

The third watercolour painting from the original C. A. Swinburne collection is titled *A Jewish King and his Page*. According to the catalogue it was commissioned in 1872 and completed in 1873. It shows an elderly heavily-robed Jewish king wearing a crown, bent over with age, resting his arm on a young man for support. It is unclear which Jewish king this painting might allude to (if any), but a painting from the same period, now in the collection of the National Gallery of Art in Washington, and titled *King Solomon*, shows remarkably similar facial features to this king. In his monograph on Solomon, published in 1985, Simon Reynolds called this painting 'a study in youth and age' and perhaps the visual metaphor here is that the old king is clinging on to youth as he grasps the young man's arm. [29] However, because of the appearance in the painting of Solomon's crystal globe motif there also might be a less obvious reading. The young page gazes into the globe which the king grasps in his left hand. With his right hand on the page's arm he draws him close encouraging him to view the 'visions' within it. Solomon's 'visions', as already suggested, are

Simeon Solomon
Greeks Going to a Festival
1873
Watercolour and gouache
on paper, 23 x 23 cm
Lane Gift, 1912

designed to satisfy the 'yearnings' of the viewer by a gradual process of enlightenment, and an acquiring of the concept of the 'Very Love' – or the artist's embodiment of male-male desire. Perhaps then there are also echoes in this painting of the Greek homoerotic concept of the pairing of an older, wiser man with a younger male in order to educate, mentor and romance him, an idea that Solomon and his circle were familiar with.[30]

The fourth painting from the C.A. Swinburne collection is *Greeks Going to a Festival*, this time recorded as being both commissioned and painted in 1873. It shows two figures striding purposefully forwards side-by-side with much billowing and flowing drapery, and there is a sense of energy about the painting which is absent from the other three works. The figure on the right holds a tall metallic-looking vase or urn, the shape of which suggests that this might be a Greek lekythos, used for storing oils for ceremonial purposes. Typical of Solomon's work from this later period, lengths of excess material are loosely looped, tied and bound around the waists, arms and necks of the figures. We know that Solomon and Algernon Swinburne shared sado-masochistic imagery, texts and fantasies with each other and implied images of binding and flagellation occur in the artist's allegorical poem as well as many of his drawings and paintings. Indeed, Solomon had already created illustrations for Swinburne's pornographic manuscript 'Lesbia Brandon' in 1865, with images of flogging and bondage.[31] In addition, there are some clues to the potential subject of the painting. The first comes from the diaries of artist George Price Boyce, a contemporary and friend of Solomon's older brother Abraham.[32] Boyce recalled attending Royal Academician Frederick Leighton's house in 1866 with Solomon, accompanied by Rossetti and Rossetti's younger brother William to see Leighton's latest large picture of *Young Greeks in Procession to Sacrifice to Diana*.[33] The painting is typical of the dawning Aesthetic movement's interest in theatrical procession and music, combining pagan sensuality with classical reason. The theme would correspond with Solomon's own Aesthetic sensibilities and his appropriation of Classical Greek myth. However, the second clue is linked more closely with Solomon and Swinburne's mutual interest in sado-masochism. In 1788, Jean Jacques Barthelemy published an imagined travel journey of the Greek Anarchasis the Younger which told of the protagonist's journey to a festival at the Temple of Diana whereupon Spartan youths were beaten on the altar of Diana 'until their blood gushed forth'.[34] This passage follows the Greek story of the Diamastigosis, a solemn ritual performed at the festival of the goddess Artemis Orthia or the Roman equivalent, Diana. The book (which it is suggested was the inspiration for the new cult of the antique in the late eighteenth century) and the story of the Diamastigsis itself will have been shared by the classically educated Swinburne with Solomon, who as a Jew, had not received the same Classical education. The imagery from the Diamastigsis can be difficult and disturbing to contemplate, but certainly it was one that Solomon had visited before in his artwork.

Between 1865 and 1867 the artist drew a series of twenty sketches which was privately published later in 1868.[35] Three of the drawings, including *Spartan Boys About to be Scourged at the Temple of Diana*, almost certainly refer to the events surrounding the Diamastigsis.[36] The twenty sketches were dedicated to Solomon and Swinburne's friend, the Welsh art collector George Powell, and the three men, with their shared interest in the works of the Marquis de Sade suggested, in the same year, (the fifty-fourth anniversary of de Sade's death), that they should devise some appropriate ceremony to celebrate this event 'like the rites of Artemis Orthia'.[37] The suggestion that the painting *Greek's Going to a Festival* might allude to this sado-masochistic event from Greek myth might still be unpalatable to some. As Gayle Seymour, in her PhD thesis on Solomon suggests, the artist was likely attempting to find 'ancient precedent' for his interest in sado-masochism, and in doing so 'revive an aura of dignity the Ancient world sometimes conferred upon such practices'.[38]

The four paintings were originally hung in C. A. Swinburne's home in Maida Vale, London, however, from around the 1880s they were moved to the barrister's new large detached residence, Beech Hurst in Andover. We know from Swinburne's catalogue where each painting was hung. *A Jewish King and his Page* and *Greeks Going to a Festival* were hung in Swinburne's drawing room alongside works by Turner, Rossetti, Poynter, Millais and others demonstrating that the barrister considered Solomon's paintings to be of equivalent aesthetic value to their more celebrated neighbours. The *Bride* and *Bridegroom* were hung in C. A. Swinburne's dining room alongside a work by Turner. The barrister said of the *Bride* and *Bridegroom* that the 'drawing, colouring, and composition' was 'exceptionally good' and, 'if not quite after the manner of the conventional treatment of sacred subjects,' they were 'still natural and original.'[39]

The paintings remained on show in the main reception rooms of C. A. Swinburne's homes from their completion in 1873 until the barrister's death in 1904. That C. A. Swinburne was happy to continue with commissioning the paintings and was not averse to displaying Solomon's work for the next thirty years in those rooms in his house where presumably he did most of his entertaining is laudable, given Solomon's arrest and subsequent notoriety, although it is difficult to say whether he would have been aware of the paintings' homoerotic and sado-masochistic allusions. It also says much about Solomon's robustness that he continued to produce paintings after his arrest that represented a sustained re-thinking about same-sex love and its implicit challenge to the heterosexual norm. Indeed, despite the fact that Solomon was almost certainly working on these paintings both before and after his arrest and subsequent release from prison and a spell in private mental asylums, he was continuing to produce work that dealt with his sexual identity.

In addition to the four works produced for C. A. Swinburne in 1873, Solomon went on to produce at least another five paintings. Despite his arrest and imprisonment for three months in Paris a year later, the artist completed another seven works. These have titles such as *Love Confronted by Death* and *Until the Day Break and the Shadows Flee Away*. They pursue the theme of androgyny and same-sex love through Solomon's unique 'vision,' played out in his allegorical prose poem and a re-interpretation of the biblical Song of Song. Despite spending nearly half his life living in poverty, Solomon would outlive a host of other artists, Aesthetes, collectors and former patrons including Rossetti, Count Stenbock and Oscar Wilde, who would bemoan the loss of his Solomon pictures in his long letter to Lord Alfred Douglas, published as

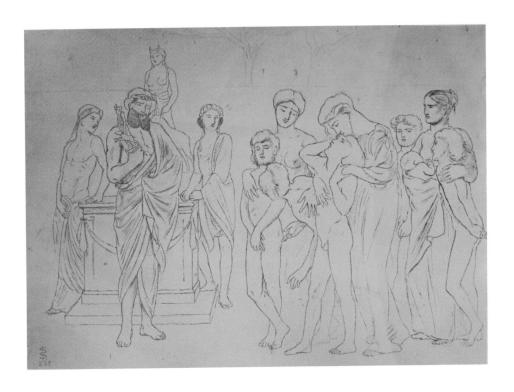

Simeon Solomon *Spartan Boys About to be Scourged at the Temple of Diana*
1862
Drawing, privately published in *Simeon Solomon, Twenty Sketches* (1868)
Mark Samuels Lasner Collection, University of Delaware Library

De Profundis, in 1897.[40] Instead, Solomon continued to live in the St Giles area of London in conditions of hardship, poverty and illness until, on the morning of 14 August 1905, he died in the dining area of the Endell Street Workhouse. He would, however, leave behind a legacy of some five-hundred-plus paintings and drawings all executed after his arrest in 1873.

The six Solomon works in the Hugh Lane collection are an important part of a greater legacy to a man who defied the conventions of respectable middle-class Victorian life. While these works are not easily decipherable because of their highly personal meaning and private mythology and symbolism, they communicated and promoted the message of male-male love at a time when it was both illegal and dangerous to be a homosexual man.

ENDNOTES

1   Lady Augusta Gregory, *Hugh Lane's Life and Achievement, with Some Account of the Dublin Galleries* (London, 1921), 56

2   Ibid.

3   James Pethica, (ed.), *Lady Gregory's Diaries, 1892-1902* (Oxford, 1996).

4   Gregory, *Hugh Lane's Life and Achievement, with Some Account of the Dublin Galleries.*

5   Christie, Manson and Woods. 'Sale of the late Charles Alfred Swinburne JP, Beech Hurst, Andover, Collection of Paintings', 2 July 1904.

6   Oscar Wilde, "The Grosvenor Gallery," *Dublin University Magazine* 90 (1877), 126.

7   William Michael Rossetti, "The Fine Art of 1858 Oil Pictures," *Saturday Review of Politics, Literature, Science and Art* 5, no. 133 (1858), 502.

8   W. M. Thackeray, "Roundabout Papers (V): Thorns in a Cushion," *Cornhill Magazine* 2 (1860). Burne-Jones quoted in G. C. Williamson, *Murray Marks and His Friends* (London, 1919), 158.

9   Robert Buchanan, "The Fleshly School of Poetry: Mr D. G. Rossetti," *Contemporary Review*, no. 18 (1871), 339.

10   Cecil. Y. Lang, ed. *The Swinburne Letters (1854-1869),* 6 vols., vol. I (New Haven, 1959), 159.

11   "The Queen vs. George Roberts and Simeon Solomon, Middlesex Sessions," *London Metropolitan Archive* (London, 1873).

12   "Pédérasts et Divers," *Les Archives du Musee de la Prefecture de Police, Paris* (Paris, 1874).

13   C. Y. Lang, ed. *The Swinburne Letters (1877 - 1882),* 6 vols., vol. IV (New Haven, 1961).

14   Charles Alfred Swinburne, *A Descriptive Catalogue of a Collection of Water-Colour Pictures and Painter-Etchers' Art at Beech-Hurst, Andover with Observations Thereon, Cursive and Discursive* (London, 1900).

15   Ibid.

16   Ibid.

17   Ibid.

18   Solomon created another watercolour version of these paintings also in 1873, this time with both parts combined into one painting. Its title is again taken from the Song of Songs: *It is the Voice of my Beloved that Knocketh.* Current location is unknown.

19   Simeon Solomon, "Letter from Simeon Solomon to Frederick Leyland," in *Pennell Collection* (Library of Congress, Washington DC).

20   Thais E Morgan, "Reimagining Masculinity in Victorian Criticism: Swinburne and Pater," in *Sexualities in Victorian Britain*, (eds.), J. E. Adams and A. H. Miller (Bloomington, 1996), 315.

21   Simeon Solomon, *A Vision of Love Revealed in Sleep* (London, 1871).

22   *Ibid.,* 1.

23   *Ibid.*

24   Ibid., 12.

25   "Letter from Simeon Solomon to Frederick Leyland."

26   Solomon, *A Vision of Love Revealed in Sleep,* 1871, 7.

27   Eric Stanilaus Stenbock, *Myrtle, Rue and Cypress* (1883, London, 1992).

28   *Ibid.*

29   Simon Reynolds, *The Vision of Simeon Solomon* (Stroud, 1985), pl. 65.

30   See Ian Anstruther, *Oscar Browning: A Biography* (London, 1983) for more on Browning and Solomon's mutual interest in what was then termed 'Greek love.'

31   A. C Swinburne, "Lesbia Brandon: An Unfinished Novel by A. C. Swinburne," in *Ashley Collection* (British Library, 1864-1866). Six of these sketches still exist in private collections, in the British Library and the Princeton University Library collections.

32   Virginia Surtees, (ed.), *The Diaries of George Price Boyce* (Norfolk, 1980).

33   Ibid.

34   Jean Jacques Barthelemy, *The Travels of Anacharsis the Younger in Greece,* 7 vols., vol. IV (London and Dublin, 1788).

35   In the collection of Mark Samuels Lasner at the University of Delaware. See Carolyn Conroy "'Images of Desire': *Twenty Sketches* by Simeon Solomon (1868)." *Pre-Raphaelite Society Review* XXIV, no. 3 (Autumn 2016).

36   The other drawings are *The Priest of Artemis* and *Mastigophorus, the Whip Bearer.* See Seymour (1986), 104-109.

37   Cecil. Y. Lang, ed. *The Swinburne Letters (1854-1869),* 6 vols., vol. I (New Haven, 1959), 312.

38   G. M. Seymour, "The Life and Work of Simeon Solomon (1840-1905)" (Santa Barbara, 1986), 105.

39   Swinburne, *A Descriptive Catalogue of a Collection of Water-Colour Pictures and Painter-Etchers' Art at Beech-Hurst, Andover with Observations Thereon, Cursive and Discursive.*

40   Oscar Wilde, *De Profundis* (London, 1905).

Édouard Manet *La Musique aux Tuileries*
1862
Oil on canvas, 76.2 x 118.1 cm
Sir Hugh Lane Bequest, 1917
The National Gallery, London

Painting Modern Paris with an eye on Past Masters: Hugh Lane's choice of Édouard Manet's *La Musique aux Tuileries* (1862)

SINÉAD FURLONG-CLANCY

Introduction

Édouard Manet's *La Musique aux Tuileries* (1862), with its depiction of contemporary figures and fashions *en plein air* and its daring, out-of-focus, loose brushwork in the centre of the canvas, is considered by many art historians to be the first significant painting of nineteenth-century Parisian modernity and the precursor of Impressionism.[1] It might therefore be thought of as a surprising acquisition by Hugh Lane, whose principal area of art dealing was Old Master paintings. In the early years of the twentieth century, when avant-garde art was only beginning to enter public collections, Manet's *La Musique aux Tuileries* was acquired by Lane in 1906 from the important Parisian art dealer and gallerist Paul Durand-Ruel, whom Lane had met in Paris in 1904. Lane acquired the work for his planned Municipal Gallery of Modern Art in Dublin, which opened in temporary premises in Harcourt Street in January 1908.

As regards the painting's provenance, Durand-Ruel recalled having purchased the work directly from Manet's studio following his now famous visit in January 1872 when, in a coup for the artist, he bought 23 paintings, spending 35,000 francs in one day.[2] Prior to this, the dealer had visited the studio of successful artist Alfred Stevens, where he had seen two paintings by Manet, *Le Saumon* and *Clair de lune sur le port de Boulogne*. At the time, Manet was having trouble selling his work, and thought that by depositing two pictures at Stevens's studio, they might attract a buyer. Upon viewing, Durand-Ruel immediately wished to purchase them and subsequently visited Manet's studio; however, in spite of his recollections, *La Musique aux Tuileries* was not noted in the inventory of that day's sale, and the work appears to have remained in Manet's possession until it was sold on 1 January 1883 – according to a note in Manet's *carnet* – to the celebrated baritone and art collector Jean-Baptiste Faure, from whom Durand-Ruel then acquired the work in 1898.[3] It remained in the dealer's stock until Lane's acquisition of it eight years later. The painting had a prominent place at Durand-Ruel's now celebrated Grafton Galleries exhibition in London in 1905, and Lane's acquisition followed in 1906.[4]

In 1906, Lane also acquired Manet's full-length portrait of Eva Gonzalès (also exhibited at the Grafton Galleries), with its established sense of contemporary portraiture more in keeping with Lane's Old Masters background. This smaller, more modern and daring work, depicting an urban crowd in an outdoor setting in Paris in 1862, was a completely different proposition. However, it bore many of the hallmarks of Manet's borrowing from past aesthetic tradition in his representation of a new modernity – a new modernity composed of a social scene out-of-doors, peopled with Manet's friends, family, fellow artists, cultural figures and acquaintances, a fashionable crowd, in Paris's public Tuileries gardens – and thus *La Musique aux Tuileries* may be considered a nod to past masters by the hand of a modern master in the making.

The Municipal Gallery of Modern Art, Dublin

Lane's determination to found a collection of modern art 'for Ireland' was inspired by his aunt Augusta, Lady Gregory, who, through her contacts, had found him his early apprenticeship at the well-known dealer Martin Colnaghi's in London, and whose circle included the poet W. B. Yeats.[5] Gregory was at the forefront of the Irish Literary Revival, most notably in terms of her involvement with the nascent National Theatre, The Abbey.[6] The crystallisation of Lane's municipal gallery idea occurred after he visited an exhibition of John Butler Yeats and Nathaniel Hone's work in Dublin in 1901, which was organised by artist Sarah Purser, who was to become one of Lane's chief supporters.[7] Lane subsequently commissioned John Butler Yeats to paint a series of portraits of national figures, and in 1904 organised an exhibition of Irish art at the Guildhall in London, which was the point of departure for a friendship and fruitful working relationship with the artist William Orpen, who subsequently acted as advisor to Lane, and with whom Lane travelled to Paris and Madrid in the spring of 1904.[8] It was during this Paris visit that Orpen brought Lane to Durand-Ruel's galleries, where Lane encountered the work of Manet and the Impressionists. By this stage, Impressionism was three decades old, and the period during which the group had staged their joint independent exhibitions (in which Manet never participated, preferring the forum of the official

Salon) was long past – eight 'Impressionist' exhibitions were held in total, the first in 1874, the last in 1886, at which Georges Seurat's pointillism heralded a new direction for avant-garde art.

After meeting Durand-Ruel and seeing his stock, Lane was immediately keen to acquire examples of modern continental painting for his Irish municipal gallery. With the idea of bringing works to Dublin to encourage purchases and donations for the collection, Lane borrowed nineteen works from Durand-Ruel for an exhibition in Dublin in November 1904 (followed by another in 1905 and a third in Belfast in 1906).[9] Among the works were two paintings by Manet, three by Claude Monet, and one by Camille Pissarro, of which one of the Manets was purchased, the portrait of Eva Gonzalès, together with Pissarro's *Spring: View* of *Louveciennes* and Monet's *Waterloo Bridge* (the latter purchased not by Lane but by Mrs Ella Fry, to donate to Lane's gallery). As noted above, *La Musique aux Tuileries*, having been exhibited at the Grafton Galleries, was acquired by Lane in 1906. By 1908, Lane had amassed a collection of 300 works, of which over one-third were presented by him as gifts or were on loan from his collection; nearly one-third had been presented by Irish and international artists, and the remaining third were donated by a 'distinguished and varied body of supporters.'[10] His extraordinary generosity was enriched by the support of artists and donors in presenting works for what is believed to the first gallery of modern art anywhere in the world.[11]

Manet's *La Musique aux Tuileries* pinpoints a key moment in the development of the aesthetic avant-garde; art historians have treated Manet's style and subject matter as the beginning of a new avant-garde, a modernity which, pre-dating Impressionism, is rooted in both the past and the present of nineteenth-century Paris. Manet brings together past aesthetic traditions and present socialising, fashions, people – filling his canvas with groups of his social, family and artistic circles. His technique not only draws the viewer's attention to the artifice of painting, it directs our eye to multiple viewpoints, multiple perspectives, as if we too were part of the proposed narrative of the canvas, the extended pictorial space encompassing our positioning as viewers of the canvas. The centre-ground, with its blurry forms in flux, may perplex, but also reminds the viewer of the approach of one's friends and acquaintances in public spaces, where light, movement and shadows make it difficult to determine identity – in much the same way that Marcel Proust's narrator experiences in the viewing of his beloved grandmother on his return to her apartment after an absence. For an instant, but only an instant, he sees what she is in purely physical terms: *une vieille femme accablée que je ne connaissais pas.*[12] Of course, this abstract sense of shapes is only momentary; as soon as the figure whom we know is recognised, the abstract apprehension of a body or grouping of bodies, hats, coats, shawls, dissipates and is replaced with our private, subjective, sense of that person.

As part of this ludic inclusion of the viewer in the extended imaginary pictorial space, the question of the music of the title comes into play. Where is the music, or those who are making it? It would seem that the artist and viewer are positioned in the place of the bandstand, where the musicians of the military bands which played regularly in public parks would be located. The viewer is positioned where the music of the title is coming from, while there is also a music that the viewer can imagine emanating from the chatter of friends, acquaintances, colleagues under the Watteauesque trees of Manet's Tuileries, in an updated rendering of the *fête champêtre*. Manet's modernity – the fashions, children, personalities, people, family groupings, an afternoon in the park – is fleeting, but also made permanent through his depiction in this painting. What could be more modern than multiple points of view, of focus, in one canvas? From the highly rendered left side of the painting, where Manet positions himself in a self-portrait next to his friend and fellow artist Albert de Balleroy, which directly echoes Les Petits Cavaliers then attributed to Velásquez (where Velázquez appears next to Murillo), which he had copied in the Louvre in 1859, to the centre-ground with its rapid brushwork which nods in the direction of Impressionism, this work contains within it both the grounding of aesthetic tradition and a desire for experimentation and the pushing of boundaries.

Painting *La Musique aux Tuileries*

La Musique aux Tuileries was painted in 1862, when Manet was thirty – and, as a point of comparison, many of the younger artists soon to be called Impressionist – Monet, Berthe Morisot, Pierre-Auguste Renoir – were in their early twenties. Manet had spent six years studying in the atelier of Thomas Couture and had travelled to copy Old Masters in museums in Europe, including spending two periods in Italy, notably returning from Florence with a study of Titian's *Venus of Urbino*, which is taken to be the starting point for *Olympia,* his controversial painting of a contemporary Parisian prostitute, painted in 1863 (Salon of 1865).[13]

By 1862, the Second Empire urbanisation of the city under Napoleon III's Prefect of the Seine, Georges-Eugène Haussmann, with its new long wide boulevards linking points of the compass, power, and transportation, had led to the creation of new public parks across the city, from the re-landscaping of the Bois de Boulogne and Bois de

Edouard Manet *Les Petits Cavaliers*
c. 1860
Oil on canvas, 45.7 x 75.6 cm
Chrysler Museum of Art, Norfolk, Virginia.
Gift of Walter P. Chrysler Jr.

Vincennes to the creation of inner-city parks and squares at the intersections of new boulevards. This was to change the nature of socialising in Paris, and the administration hoped that it would both bring light and air into the heart of Paris, create socialising spaces, and be a stabilising feature to the communities in each *quartier*, not to mention less easy to barricade in times of possible further civil unrest and revolution. In 1860, Paris had annexed the outer-lying communes such as Belleville, and the twenty *arrondissements* that we know today were delineated.[14]

Into this new urban scene, Manet emerged from his studies at Couture's atelier, and at the Louvre, where he had been copying since the early 1850s. In 1859 he had made a copy of *Les Petits Cavaliers*, then attributed to Velásquez, in the Louvre, in which a group of gentlemen – *une réunion de treize personnages*, as the subtitle has it – can be seen as a precursor to Manet's *La Musique aux Tuileries*. Manet's copy, entitled

Les Petits Cavaliers, is now in the Chrysler Museum of Art. It reveals Manet's interest in colour and tone as well as subject and composition. While his early Salon submissions clearly reveal an Old Master influence, he was also keen to learn from modern masters. Accompanied by a fellow student, Antonin Proust, he visited Eugène Delacroix in 1854-55 with the pretext of obtaining permission to copy Delacroix's *La Barque de Dante*, which hung in the Musée du Luxembourg.[15] The influence of Delacroix is evident in Manet's copy of the *Petits Cavaliers*. In terms of his fledgling career, Manet's first submission to the Paris Salon, in 1859, *Le Buveur d'absinthe*, had been rejected. However, Manet's portrait of his parents, *Portrait de M. et Mme Auguste Manet*, and his *Chanteur Espagnole* were accepted for the Salon de 1861 and with his success, Manet gained a following.

At the time, the Tuileries gardens were a centre of sociability and elegant promenading. During the summer of 1862, Manet spent his afternoons sketching in the Tuileries, often in the company of his friend, poet and prose writer Charles Baudelaire. In his pen and wash sketches, Manet captured the essence of modern socialising by concentrating on lines and forms, and restricting detail to a minimum, in much the same way as popular illustrator Constantin Guys did. In Baudelaire's essay *Le Peintre de la vie moderne* (written in late 1859 and early 1860, but not published until 1863), Baudelaire makes Guys his 'painter of modern life', using Guys's illustrations of modern Paris as a starting point for his essay on *la modernité*.[16] An analysis of Manet's ink and wash studies, the *Fiacre*, *Équipage* and the *Tuileries* conserved in the Cabinet des Estampes of the Bibliothèque Nationale, clearly reveals the influence of Guys, as does the preparatory study *Étude pour La Musique aux Tuileries* (1862, private collection) pairing Suzanne Leenhoff and Eugène Manet very similarly to the final composition, as discussed below.[17] Manet, like Baudelaire, had a collection of Guys's watercolours depicting Parisian 'high life'.[18]

In order to create images of contemporary Paris, Manet took on the role of illustrator, observing the fleeting social interaction of both adults and children in the Tuileries in preparation for painting *La Musique aux Tuileries*.[19] This was something new for Manet; he preferred to work in his studio rather than embrace the *plein-airisme* adopted by the Impressionists. But the preparatory studies for the Tuileries painting reveal the sense of an alternative tradition – popular illustration – that became the process of painting his own version of modern life in the modestly sized *La Musique aux Tuileries* (76 x 118 cm) before making his modernity the equivalent of History painting in his large scale canvases

Constantin Guys *Meeting in the Park*
Pen and brown ink, grey, blue and black wash, 21.7 x 30cm
Metropolitan Museum of Art, New York
Rogers Fund, 1937

Le Déjeuner sur l'herbe (208 x 264 cm, originally 214 x 270 cm[20]) and *Olympia* (130.5 x 190 cm) of 1863.

In *La Musique aux Tuileries* the sense of an outdoor social world has echoes of the French eighteenth-century artist Antoine Watteau, who painted many scenes of outdoor socialising, the *fête champêtre*, of elegant men, women and children in fashionable dress and wooded environs,[21] such as in his *Fête galante in a Wooded Landscape*. (*c.* 1719-1721, The Wallace Collection), where the viewer can identify elements such as the arching trees, which are repeated in Manet's *Tuileries*. One can also identify in Manet's painting the aesthetic tradition of the group portrait of shared interests, which had originated in Dutch seventeenth-century painting and was 'explored extensively' in the nineteenth century,[22] and, more specifically, the group portrait of thirteen artists then attributed to Velásquez, discussed above, which Manet had copied in the Louvre, in which Velásquez appears next to Murillo.[23] In Manet's *Tuileries*, Manet situates himself within the cultured crowd, with his

88

Antoine Watteau *Fete galante in a Wooded Landscape*
c. 1719-21
Oil on canvas, 127.2 x 191.7 cm
Wallace Collection, London

friend artist Albert de Balleroy the Murillo to Manet's Velásquez, in a self-portrait cropped at the far left of the painting, the artist viewing the viewer viewing his painting.

Such aesthetic references combine in *La Musique aux Tuileries* with the contemporary fashions of mid-century Paris, with crinolines, bonnets, top hats, dominating, even cluttering, Manet's painting. Well-known literary, musical and artistic figures crowd the scene. From left to right, the figures have been identified as Édouard Manet; Albert de Balleroy; possibly the art critic and novelist Champfleury behind them; the artist Zacharie Astruc (seated); behind Astruc, the journalist Aurélien Scholl; in the foreground, Mme Lejosne (in whose home Manet had met both Bazille and Baudelaire) in bonnet and blue ribbons; behind her, in profile, Baudelaire; talking to Baudelaire, the poet Théophile Gautier, and Baron Taylor, Inspector of Museums in France;

behind Baudelaire, and to the immediate left of the tree trunk, facing the viewer, the artist Henri Fantin-Latour; in the foreground, in a veiled bonnet, Mme Offenbach, wife of the composer (also identified as Mme Loubens); to the right of the tree trunk, Suzanne Leenhoff, soon to be Manet's wife, her young son, Léon Leenhoff, Mme Manet *mère*, and Eugène Manet standing and in profile; Jacques Offenbach behind him, seated, in front of the tree trunk; Charles Monginot, artist, standing in profile and raising his top hat.[24]

As the 2013 Royal Academy exhibition *Manet: Portraying Life* set out to demonstrate, in his work, Manet places people he knows in scenes of contemporary life: in *La Musique aux Tuileries*, we view an assembled cast of Manet's friends, fellow artists, cultural figures and family. His portraits within his paintings of modern life reveal his solidity, of both vision and execution; his desire to reference past models – particularly Velásquez and Hals – and to become a part of that Old Master tradition while representing his own cultural moment. Far from being a prolific, rapid, illustrator as was Guys, capturing the suggestion of modern interaction in public and private spaces, Manet establishes a powerful relation between his sitters and the viewer; with his use of paint adding weight to this inescapable dynamic.

The sight lines for the Royal Academy exhibition only enhanced this aspect of Manet's work, with the walls painted a dark grey, and one room focusing the viewer's energy entirely on *La Musique aux Tuileries*, where, with the help of the viewer's key, for the first time, this writer completely understood the central suggested grouping of Manet's soon-to-be-wife Suzanne (in a veiled bonnet, black cloak and pale blue dress, with her back to us, seated on a wrought-iron chair, reading a journal), Léon, her young son looking ahead to his right and his mother, while leaning his head on Mme Manet *mère*, who is wearing a black veiled bonnet (in mourning for her husband, Manet's father), occupying the space between Suzanne and Eugène, and Eugène, the artist's brother, in top hat, leaning in to the group (Eugène's presence here has previously been well documented).[25]

Manet was concerned with rendering more than fleeting impressions, but in technical terms, in the central area of the canvas, which reveals rapid, apparently unfinished brushwork, there is a suggestion of movement, with a sketchiness of technique that evokes the fleeting moment, the contemporary fashions so heralded by Baudelaire, and the difficulties of vision – of making figures out in the mid-distance – in a scene which demands that the eye look in different directions all at once and reverses traditional assumptions about the centre of the canvas. Perhaps this also explains the difference of finish in the left side of the canvas, upon which our eye fixes easily, as opposed to the central section to which we come and go, via the figures of the fashionable women, Mme Offenbach / Mme Loubens and Mme Lejosne who face us, inscrutable, as we attempt to make out different figures one by one, but always with some difficulty.

The inability to define the nature of the complex viewing exchange and the mixed technique of *La Musique aux Tuileries* made the painting problematic for contemporary critics and viewers when it was shown in Manet's first major exhibition of fourteen pictures in the gallery of the dealer Martinet in 1863. Many were shocked by the lack of finish and the patches (*taches*) of pigment suggesting figures in the crowd. Reportedly, Delacroix, at the end of his life, wished he had gone to Manet's defence after seeing the work at Martinet's,[26] and Émile Zola did so, suggesting that, for those who were shocked by the work, one should view the painting from a 'respectful distance' where all made sense: the crowd, 'a hundred people perhaps, who are bustling around in the sun [...] [one] would see that these *taches* were alive, that the crowd was talking, and that this canvas was one of the characteristic works of the artist, the one where he has most obeyed his eyes and temperament'.[27] Baudelaire did not comment directly on the painting, and it is assumed from this that he was somehow not satisfied with it;[28] whereas Frédéric Bazille, after visiting Martinet's with Monet, who is reported to have been 'deeply impressed', wrote home enthusiastically, 'You wouldn't believe how much I am learning by looking at these pictures! One of these sessions is worth a month of work!'[29]

Manet's *La Musique aux Tuileries* is a fascinating combination of formal portraiture and informal observation and goes beyond the art-historical tendency to nominate it the precursor of Impressionism. It is weightier, more self-conscious, it acknowledges the distraction of visual attention and resulting perceptions in a crowded outdoor space (about which Jonathan Crary has so perceptively written[30]), is inclusive of family, children, fashion and play, and is more attached to an acknowledgment of past tradition than a fleeting present captured by popular illustration. The viewer is invited to engage with Manet's depiction of modernity, to look at it and to participate in the guessing game. The representation of the ephemera of modernity – Walter Benjamin's 'fossils'[31] – items of contemporary history: fashions, wrought-iron chairs, parasols, buckets and spades, seems to enthral Manet in his modern depiction, overlaid on centuries of aesthetic tradition, of the

Charles Marville *Ailée bordée d'arbres*
1850–53
Photograph, salted paper print from paper negative
Metropolitan Museum of Art, New York
Harris Brisbane Dick Fund, 1946

crowd in *La Musique aux Tuileries*. In doing so, he put contemporary fashion and urban leisure on the same level as the subjects represented in History painting. And what followed a year later, of course, was his depiction of a contemporary Parisian prostitute, *Olympia* – posed by artist, musician and model Victorine Meurent – with even more direct reference to an Old Master tradition – Titian's *Venus of Urbino* – and far more shock value.

Conclusion

Manet's blending of past and present in *La Musique aux Tuileries* surely appealed to Lane, with his expertise in Old Masters and his interest in the modern schools of Continental, British and Irish art. In the year following Lane's acquisition of the work, further value would have been added to his acquisition as the French government relocated Manet's *Olympia*, which had been purchased for the state by subscription at the behest of Monet in 1889-90, to the Louvre, the museum which exhibited and conserved works by artists who were considered worthy of the honour after ten years had elapsed following their death. Until 1907, *Olympia* was located in the Luxembourg, the museum of living artists, even though Manet had died in 1883, more than twenty years previously.[32] This move signalled Manet's formal acceptance by the French establishment as a modern master, and added an additional level of importance to Lane's acquisition of *La Musique aux Tuileries*, now acknowledged to be one of the most significant works of Parisian modernity, for his Municipal Gallery of Modern Art, Dublin.

Marino Branch
Brainse Marino
Tel: 8336297

ENDNOTES

1   For example, in the catalogue of the major centenary retrospective exhibition of 1983, *Manet: 1832-1883*, Françoise Cachin writes, 'It becomes the prototype of all Impressionist and Post-Impressionist art representing contemporary life out-of-doors and in popular public places'. Françoise Cachin, Charles S. Moffett, Michel Melot, Galeries Nationales du Grand Palais and The Metropolitan Museum Of Art, *Manet: 1832-1883* (New York, 1983), cat.38,126 (catalogue hereafter abbreviated as CMM).

2   Sylvie Patry (ed.), *Inventing Impressionism: Paul Durand-Ruel and the Modern Art Market* (London, 2015), cat. 22, 243, and CMM, cat. 118, 312.

3   CMM, cat. 38, 126. Patry, *Inventing Impressionism*, cat. 22, 243.

4   Patry, *Inventing Impressionism*, cat. 22, 243; CMM, 126.

5   Roy Foster, '"A family affair": Lane, Gregory, Yeats and educating the nation', in B. Dawson (ed.), *Hugh Lane: Founder of a Gallery of Modern Art for Ireland* (London, 2008), 18.

6   Foster, '"A family affair"', 16, and Robert O'Byrne, 'Hugh Lane: the man and his milieu' in Dawson, *Hugh Lane*, 30.

7   See 'Sarah Purser', in B. Dawson (ed.), *Images and Insights* (Dublin, 1993), 66.

8   Foster, '"A family affair"', 19; O'Byrne, 'Hugh Lane', 35.

9   Philip McEvansoneya, 'Lane's choices: Degas, Monet, Pissarro and Puvis de Chavannes', in Dawson, *Hugh Lane*, 38.

10   Jessica O'Donnell, 'Hugh Lane's vision' in Dawson, *Hugh Lane*, 49.

11   Barbara Dawson, 'Hugh Lane's pictures' in Dawson, *Hugh Lane*, 9.

12   Marcel Proust, *Le Côté de Guermantes*, I (Paris, 1987), 218.

13   Éric Darragon, *Manet* (Paris, 198), 21-29.

14   On Haussmann's transformed and newly created public parks as new urban space, see Sinéad Furlong-Clancy, *The Depiction and Description of the Female Body in French Art, Literature and Society: Women in the Parks of Paris, 1848-1900* (New York, 2014).

15   CMM, cat. 1, 45-46. Darragon, *Manet*, 31.

16   Charles Baudelaire, *Le Peintre de la vie moderne* (1863) in *Œuvres complètes*, II (Paris: Gallimard, La Pléiade, 1976), 695: 'La modernité, c'est le transitoire, le fugitif, le contingent, la moitié de l'art, dont l'autre moitié est l'éternel et l'immuable. Il y a eu une modernité pour chaque peintre ancien; la plupart des beaux portraits qui nous restent des temps antérieurs sont revêtus des costumes de leur époque'.

17   Illustrated in CMM, cat. 38, fig. a.

18   CMM, cat. 38, 124.

19   See Françoise Cachin, *Manet: 'j'ai fait ce que j'ai vu'* (Paris, 1994), 32-35.

20   CMM, cat. 62, 165.

21   David Scott, 'Framing Modern Life: Manet, Watteau and Genre Painting', illustrated lecture, Dublin City Gallery The Hugh Lane, 14 November 1999. Michael Fried notes the small children playing in the foreground of *La Musique aux Tuileries* 'may derive from any of a number of paintings by Watteau'. See Michael Fried, *Manet's Modernism, or the Face of Painting in the 1860s*, (Chicago and London,1998 (1996)), 44.

22   Mary Anne Stevens et al., *Manet: Portraying Life*, (London, 2012), cat.26, 186.

23   CMM, cat.38.

24   See Cachin (CMM, cat.38 and 1994, 34-35); Stevens, *Manet*, cat. 26, 186; Darragon, *Manet*, 62-63; David Bomford, Jo Kirby, John Leighton and Ashok Roy, *Art in the Making: Impressionism* (London, 1990), 112.

25   See previous note.

26   See CMM, cat. 38, 126.

27   Quoted in Bomford, *Art in the Making*, 119.

28   CMM, cat. 38, 126.

29   Quoted in Bomford, *Art in the Making*, 112.

30   See Jonathan Crary, *Suspensions of Perception: Attention, Spectacle, and Modern Culture* (Cambridge, Mass./ London, 1999).

31   On Benjamin's concept of industrial objects as 'fossils' (the trace of living history that can be read from the surfaces of surviving objects), see Susan Buck-Morss, *The Dialectics of Seeing: Walter Benjamin and the Arcades Project* (Cambridge, Mass./ London, 1997 (1991)), 56, 65, 285.

32   See Christopher Riopelle, 'Looking at Lane from the Continent', in Dawson, *Hugh Lane*, 46; McEvansoneya, 'Lane's choices', 38.

LOST ON THE LUSITANIA

Sir Hugh Lane.

Height about 5ft. 11in.

Build—very slight.

Hair dark brown, slightly turning grey, rather bald, small pointed beard, chest hairy.

Forehead very high, deep set eyes, large nose.

Wore cellular underclothing marked " H. Lane" and Jaeger cholera belt.

Usually wore plain gold signet ring with lion crest as shown below.

When last seen was wearing pearl tie pin.

Communicate by Wire with

CHARLES LANE,

26 South Mall, Cork.

Lost on the Lusitania
Courtesy of the National Library of Ireland

Sir Hugh Lane (1875-1915), Harold Ainsworth Peto (1854-1933), James Miller (1860-1947) and the designs of the Cunard Liners RMS *Lusitania* and RMS *Mauretania*

LYNDA MULVIN

In 1907, some years before the tragic sinking of the RMS *Lusitania* on 7 May 1915, the interior decoration and design of this great luxury liner, and that of her sister ship the RMS *Mauretania*, was undertaken by the architect Harold Ainsworth Peto (1854-1933) and James Miller (1860-1947), a Scottish architect who had previously worked on Scottish railway engineering for the Caledonian Railway Offices.[1]

From 1871, Harold Peto had enjoyed an illustrious career as an Edwardian architect and garden designer, in partnership with Ernest George. Their successful practice in London employed Edwin Landseer Lutyens (1869-1944) and Herbert Baker (1862-1946) as assistants. Coincidentally James Miller's son George would join Herbert Baker's practice in 1934. At this time these notable Edwardian architects were closely connected and together collaborated on new design ideas committed to simple aesthetics, directed towards a new modernity. Peto was influential on the work of Lutyens, who would become a friend and colleague supported by Hugh Lane.

At the turn of the 20th century, the London artistic scene was dynamic and Lane met many literary figures, contemporary artists and architects such as Lutyens. Lane's connections had been well established in Ireland through his aunt Augusta, Lady Gregory, who also provided links to the art world in London, notably with art dealer Martin Colnaghi with whom Lane worked from 1893 to 1898 before setting up his own successful art dealing business. The well-known portrait of Hugh Lane painted by Antonio Mancini in 1906 depicts Lane at the pinnacle of his career with an enviable reputation in London, where he had recently organised the first exhibition of Irish artists in the Guildhall.

William Walcott *Proposed Bridge Gallery*, distant front view
Watercolour on paper, 50.7 x 79.8 cm
Lane Bequest, 1913

Lane had a vision for a municipal modern art gallery in Dublin, to which he would donate his growing collection of modern art. Seeking a suitable site for such a gallery, Lutyens proposed replacing the pedestrian Ha'penny or Wellington Bridge over the river liffey with his Liffey Bridge Art Gallery in 1912. Although this project was never executed, the municipal gallery of modern art did open in Clonmell House in Harcourt Street, Dublin in 1908. Lutyens, who had close connections to Ireland through his Cork-born mother, did create a garden for Lane, also born in Cork, for his private residence at Cheyne Walk, London. As noted above Lutyens had previously worked with Peto, a significant connection, because Peto had, together with Miller, fitted out the *Mauretania* and *Lusitania* the liner on which Hugh Lane was sailing when it was torpedoed in 1915 causing his death.

Harold Peto's partnership with Ernest George was dissolved in 1892. Peto agreed to work on garden designs in England only[2] and from

1899 he worked on his own house and garden at Iford Manor, Wiltshire, which provided him with the ideal landscape setting for expanding his interests and ideals. He had a varied practice including his commission for a sunken garden at Garinish, West Cork for the Annan Bryce family.[3] While still concentrating on garden design, Peto had the interesting sideline of designing the interiors of the Cunard liners in 1911, which did not technically come under the umbrella of building design in England.

The *Lusitania* and *Mauretania*

The two superliners, the *Lusitania* and her running mate and sister ship, the *Mauretania*, were British ocean liners of the Cunard Line, whose company motto was 'Advancing civilisation since 1840'.[4] The ship engineering and hull designs dating from 1905 were by senior naval architect Leonard Peskett (1861-1924) with the goal of building the world's fastest liner; they would be, briefly, the world's largest passenger ships in the early 1900s.[5] The *Lusitania* made her maiden voyage from Liverpool to New York in 1907. Able to run through the water at an average of twenty-five knots, she was the holder of the Blue Riband for the fastest Atlantic crossing and became known as the 'greyhound of the seas'. There was considerable rivalry with the *Mauretania* and between them they held the Blue Riband for twenty-two years. There was stiff competition from German ships in Hamburg where the North German Lloyd shipping company's liners *Bremen* and *New York*, were direct trans-Atlantic rivals. The speed of the *Lusitania* would eventually be superseded by that of the RMS *Olympic*, and her sister ship RMS *Titanic*.

These great Cunard Line ships were named after Roman provinces of Lusitania (modern day Portugal and Spain) and Mauretania (Morocco and Algeria), located opposite each other at the Pillars of Hercules or Straits of Gibraltar.[6] Miller and Peto fitted out the interiors of the two ships accordingly: the *Lusitania* or 'Lucy', as she became fondly known, had a gold and white colour scheme visually linking the predominant colours of Spanish pueblos and Spanish baroque gold altars, while the *Mauretania*, or 'Mary', had a darker colour scheme with a profusion of natural wood and textiles to echo the Moorish connections of the North African continent.

The palatial luxurious interiors of the great liners, as fitted by Peto and Miller, were associated with opulent facilities and lifestyle: detailed advertisements survive for Turkish baths complete with barber service, private suites with plumbed bathrooms, Teutonic smoking rooms, upper saloons on deck, modern libraries, electric light fittings on all decks, as well as lengthy promenades and sheltered garden areas. The Atlantic crossing experience was designed to be majestic, speedy and elegant maintaining the standards of all the convenience of modern living combined with the service and luxury of great hotels. The decorative setting was to evoke calm European grandeur, with different ornamented settings reflecting various design trends, from French courtly interiors to the Italianate loggia for the main reception rooms, to an orangerie or outside portico, with stairs to upper levels and promenades linked to adjoining corridors. These linkages were designed to connect the public areas and private spaces to the main reception areas. The linearity of the ships' layout led to the interconnection of great dining rooms and drawing rooms, as in the design of a large hotel; light-filled rooms were powered with electric chandeliers, enabling display of the intricacy of their decorative detailing, as elaborate ceilings patterned with stuccowork drew the eye upwards.

James Miller had designed airy light train stations for West Highland Railways such as Wemyss Bay Railway Station, Firth of Clyde, in 1903. Wemyss Bay was the home of the Director of Cunard Lines and was the test area for trial speeds of many of the liners. Miller was renowned for the quality of his designs and for his output. In 1902 he also built the Town Hall in Clydebank, home of John Brown Ship Building and Engineering Ltd, shipyard of the *Lusitania*.

The *Mauretania* was built in 1906 at the shipyard of Swan Hunter in Tyneside. Peto and Miller must have discussed details of their designs, for the light and dark decorative themes of the two liners are both complementary and contrasting. It is interesting to note that surviving *Mauretania* interiors are currently at Pinewood Studios, London, purchased in the post-war years. Here an idea of the opulence of these ships' interiors can be felt: the original library from the *Mauretania* bedecks the Pinewood boardroom; the executive offices and the corridors of the studios are also all cased from the ships' fittings.[7] We can sense the degree of grandeur, illustrating Peto's interior design concept, from his fondness for carved wood, in particular on the columns flanking the library shelves. The positioning of these columns is a feature of Peto interiors. The imagery of the dolphin, carved into the wood tablet, is a reference to this sacred sea creature, the messenger of the sea god Poseidon and because Aphrodite was born out of the sea, dolphins are also closely associated with her. This dolphin motif is repeated by Peto in his work in the south of Ireland and found at Garinish in Cork, decorating the column capitals.

The bedrooms in the liners also displayed elements of tasteful design, with lavish textiles used for pelmets, furnishings and fixings. Inasmuch as these interiors could be construed in the idiom of interior design, there were naturalistic subtle muted hues and monochrome masses embracing the vista of the horizon, the sea and the wilderness of the maritime landscape. For Peto, the planned vista was a significant element in his design ideas: he worked to bring the outside in and vice versa. Soon the exotic tone of travel by luxury liner would be translated into strong motifs in details of modernist architecture.

Harold Peto turned, as we have noted, from designing ships' interiors to designing gardens: at Garinish, between 1911 and 1914, he created an exuberant garden on the hilly terrain of this windswept island, where he would revive Italianate garden tradition. In this garden, he embraced ideas of simplicity and clarity of form, employing elements chosen for their functional elegance, such as flights of steps, combining long views of valley and wilderness and faraway coastal shores, striking a balance between the formal garden and wild vegetation.[8] He purchased marbles to insert at different vantage points in his garden, incorporating structure and form and featuring antique artefacts collected on his travels. In consideration of the ships' designs, Peto embraced the rigid formality of the linear planning of vistas on the ship combined with the far off seascapes as backdrop. Similarly, the relationships of wilderness and formal architecture were present in his gardens, and his own garden at Iford Manor provides a clear picture of his visionary approach to design at this time.[9]

In the same way that he included Elizabethan oak panelling in the surrounds of the entrance to the library on the *Mauretania*, he included new and old art objects for symbolic reasons in his garden designs. These structured vistas were an important element of Peto's design – the aspect of the shaded 'cosy corners' with ashlar walls, studded with marble treasures arranged in chronological sequence. Such types of screen fitments and 'cosy corners' were commonly found in Edwardian architectural interiors; Peto extended this design idea of separate aspects and boundaries from house to garden.[10] In this way, by combining structure with symbiotic planting, he brought the interior to the exterior, and, as with his designs for the *Mauretania* interiors, he aspired to create seamless inside/outside public spaces.

His progressive attitude bridged the transition from Victorian eclecticism and the Arts and Crafts movement towards Modernism, where architecture became the underlying structure, combined with antique sculpture. As a collector he viewed the antiquities as 'revelation of authenticity of the sacred nature of the object as originally crafted by master masons and craftsmen and as artistic art objects'.[11] This is in keeping with the ideals of the Arts and Craft movement, as he describes, 'These bits of old sculpture, I feel, are so much more as the artist'; he collected artefacts from various sources in Italy and France and wrote how the supply of antiquities was dwindling away and 'probably before long they will be unobtainable'. [12]

Commissioning the leading architects and engineers of the time to fit out the Cunard liners was a progressive approach. It ensured that the fresh design concepts which were being applied to contemporary houses and gardens were also adapted to the modernity of design in these great vessels. These sleek machines were transportation models for the future, incorporating the latest form of transport and attracting a new genre of traveller to these luxury liners.

As World War I gripped Europe, the waters around Ireland and Great Britain were to become treacherous. As the mail boats, passenger ships and supply ships continued to ply the ocean between Europe and America, German U-boats looked for targets. The shipping lanes from New York to Liverpool went via Queenstown (now Cobh) in Cork. After a short period in New York, on the first of May 1915, Hugh Lane took a first class passage on the *Lusitania* bound for Liverpool. As the *Lusitania* was steaming towards Queenstown harbour, five days into the voyage, she was torpedoed by the German U20 boat, and sank in less than eighteen minutes off Old Kinsale Head.[13] She was carrying approximately 1900 passengers, including Hugh Lane; more than 1200 passengers and crew perished that disastrous day.[14] Hugh Lane was a progressive leading art connoisseur who moved between London, Dublin and New York using this modern form of transport on the Atlantic prestige route; on his last voyage he was transporting works of art intended for his Dublin art gallery, only to be tragically lost at sea in an untimely death.

Hugh Lane's passing is marked by the celebration of this Decade of Centenaries and by the many thousands who visit the artworks on display in Dublin City Gallery The Hugh Lane every year – a small token of gratitude to this remarkable visionary man, who created the first public art gallery in the world in the Municipal Gallery of Modern Art, now known as Dublin City Gallery The Hugh Lane.

ENDNOTES

1   J. Kent Layton, *Lusitania: An Illustrated Biography* (Stroud, 2019).

2   H. J. Grainger, 'Harold A. Peto (1854-1933), architect, interior designer, collector and aesthete', in Christopher Webster (ed.), *The Practice of Architecture: eight architects, 1830-1930* (London, 2012), 169-205; Robin Whalley, *The Great Edwardian Gardens of Harold Peto* (London, 2007) and Audrey Sloan and Gordon Murray, *James Miller: 1860–1947* (Edinburgh, 1993).

3   Lynda Mulvin, *Harold Ainsworth Peto (1854-1933) and the Annan Bryce Marble Sculpture Collection at Garinish Ilnacullin Island Garden, Co. Cork, Ireland* (Dublin, 2015); Whalley, *The Great Edwardian Gardens*, 122-39; Nigel Everett, *Wild Gardens: The Lost Demesnes of Bantry Bay* (Bantry, 2000) and N. Everett, 'Island Paradise', *Irish Arts Review*, vol. 30 (2013). See also A.G.L. Hellyer, 'A garden in search of a house', *Country Life*, vol. 138 (11 March 1965), 512-14. During his life Peto travelled to Europe, USA and Japan and wrote diaries concurrently and was a great admirer of the Italian Renaissance and the Italianate garden; R. Whalley, *Harold Peto Travel Diaries 4: France and Italy 1889* (Cwareli Press, 2013). He had several active garden commissions including the gardens at Buscot Park (1906), West Dean (1910) in England and Isola Bella in Cannes on the French Riviera (1910). See also Whalley, *The Great Edwardian Gardens*, 140-58 and David Ottewill, *The Edwardian Garden* (New Haven and London, 1989), 156-58.

4   Peter Newall, *Mauretania: Triumph and Resurrection* (Manchester, 2006).

5   David Ramsay, *The Lusitania Saga & Myth 100 years on* (South Yorkshire, 2015), 80. For details about Leonard Peskett see online resource Graces Naval history http://www.gracesguide.co.uk/Leonard_Peskett

6   These evocative names had a precedent in the Cunard Line with earlier pairs of paddle steamships named Etruria and Umbria and the Campania and Lucania. See http://whitestarmoments.weebly.com.

7   http://maritimematters.com/2013/07/pinewood-with-peter-seeking-out-mauretania-in-movieland/

8   Ottewill, *The Edwardian Garden*, 146-58, and E. Malins and P. Bowe, *Irish Gardens and Demesnes from 1830* (London, 1980), 95-100.

9   Whalley, *The Great Edwardian Gardens*, 158-85.

10 Helen Long, *The Edwardian House: The Middle-Class Home in Britain 1880-1914* (Manchester, 1993), 170-71.

11 Harold Peto, *The Boke of Iford compiled by me Harold Peto of Iford Manor from all the sources available in 1917*, with an historical introduction by Robin Whalley (Marlborough, England: Libanus Press, 1993), 46.

12 ibid.

13 The U-boat was captained by Walther Schwieger. The ship's log details how at 3pm the *Lusitania* turned starboard to head for Queenstown. She was hit with a torpedo and a subsequent explosion ripped the bulkheads apart.

14 Crucially for historical events, many of the civilians who perished were US citizens. Seen as the turning point in World War I, this was the event that drew in the USA on the side of the Allied forces.

Opening of Johannesburg Art Gallery, November 1910

Lane, Lutyens and the Johannesburg Art Gallery

JILLIAN CARMAN

Hugh Lane was one of the most important curators in the early twentieth century. In just over six years he established three museums: two municipal galleries of modern art in Dublin (January 1908) and Johannesburg (November 1910), and a national museum of seventeenth-century Dutch and Flemish paintings, The Michaelis Collection, in Cape Town (May 1914).[1] This essay focuses on Lane's foundation collection for Johannesburg and its purpose-designed Edwin Lutyens building.[2]

Both the Dublin and Johannesburg collections were housed in temporary premises when they opened, and both were considered by British avant-garde critics to contain exceptional examples of modern art by British and French[3] artists who were not represented in British institutions. The Johannesburg collection was exhibited to great acclaim in London (May-June and July 1910) before being shipped to South Africa in September 1910. The choice of exhibition venue, the Whitechapel Art Gallery in the impoverished East End of London, was considered regrettable as 'would-be colonizers of Darkest London'[4] from the West End had to make a pilgrimage to get there – 'it is a far cry to Whitechapel', lamented Martin Hardie (1910)[5] – and Whitechapel inhabitants were unlikely to appreciate the art.[6] The choice of South Africa as the ultimate destination was even worse, a colonial backwater devoid of any form of culture 'where pictures are virtually unknown' in the opinion of the critic Charles Hind (1910). [7] One senses that Dublin was also considered an unfortunate place for modern art, akin to an unappreciative colony.

Johannesburg was more fortunate than Dublin in that the architect of Lane's choice, Edwin Lutyens, was appointed and his partially built gallery opened in 1915. Dublin was not so lucky. Lutyens was rejected and Hugh Lane's collection never received a purpose-designed building. So, while both institutions marked the centenary in 2015 of

Installation view of founding collection 2014

Lane's death, Johannesburg also celebrated the centenary of the opening of its collection in a permanent home in Joubert Park, the only museum that Lutyens ever designed and built in his long career.

The much smaller Johannesburg collection is similar to Dublin's but it differs in a number of areas.[8] The emphasis in Johannesburg is on British rather than Irish artists and, whereas Dublin promoted national artists, Johannesburg did not. Lane had a clean slate in Johannesburg: he did not have to build on an existing nucleus like Dublin's Staats Forbes collection 'which favoured Constable, Corot and Millet'.[9] Nor did he have to scratch for funds or deal with a recalcitrant town council because Florence Phillips, South African-born wife of the mining magnate Sir Lionel Phillips and the driving force behind the founding and funding of the Johannesburg Art Gallery, supervised these tasks.[10] In addition, Lane had almost complete curatorial autonomy.[11]

Perhaps the most important difference between the two galleries, however, is the context in which each was founded. Lane's Irish project can be seen as part of the great Irish theatrical and literary revival of the late nineteenth to early twentieth century, into which he was drawn through his beloved aunt Augusta, Lady Gregory, and his friendship with William Butler Yeats and others. He was not particularly literary himself and seems to have been politically naïve, or at least apolitical, seemingly unaware of the literary circle's anti-British sentiments during the recent South African War (1899-1902).[12] But, as he said at the time

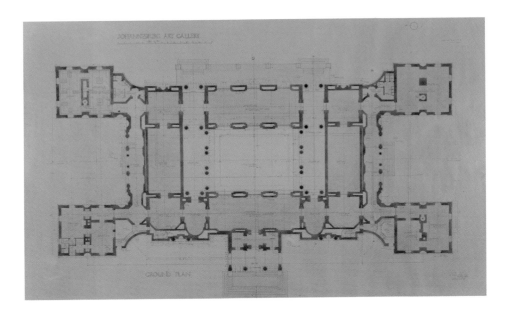

Edwin Lutyens' ground plan for the Johannesburg Art Gallery

to George Moore, 'I am Lady Gregory's nephew, and must be doing something for Ireland'.[13]

Johannesburg's gallery emerged in a context of reconstruction after a devastating civil war, the South African (or Anglo-Boer) War of 1899 to 1902 between the English and the Afrikaans.[14] The victorious English, who took possession of Johannesburg in 1900, immediately set about some social engineering under Alfred Milner: the enticement of English families to settle in Johannesburg, creating a stable community that would shore up British colonial rule and service the mines.[15] Prior to the war, Johannesburg, which was founded in 1886 with the discovery of gold, was regarded as an inadequately developed town unsuitable for family life. Though there were pockets of domesticity, single men and prostitutes were a prominent social feature.[16] There was little governance structure and the town had to defer in all matters to the seat of government of the Boer (or Transvaal) Republic in Pretoria. Under the English, central governance moved from Pretoria to Johannesburg, which gradually transformed into a stable, attractive town with civic buildings and cultural amenities for families. Florence

Johannesburg Art Gallery south façade

and Lionel Phillips returned to settle in this developing town in 1906, with frequent journeys 'home'. They had been in exile during the South African War – banished because of Lionel's implication in the infamous Jameson Raid of 1895-96, one of the principal causes of the war.[17] Their exile was spent in the comfort of their London home in Grosvenor Square and their lavish country estate in Hampshire, Tylney Hall.

On her return to Johannesburg, Florence immediately became involved in reconstructive charitable initiatives, encouraging local arts and crafts projects such as home industries and the manufacture and sale of South African goods to provide much-needed employment.[18] She became a leading figure in the Johannesburg branch of the South African National Union (SANU), which had been established towards the end of 1907 to promote South African goods. In order to encourage local manufacture, ranging from furniture through metalwork to needlecraft, a major arts and crafts exhibition was planned for early 1910, under the control of SANU's Johannesburg Ladies' Committee. This is when the seed of the Johannesburg Art Gallery was planted. The arts and crafts exhibition was to display the finest examples of handcrafts to act as teaching models for the locals. Some of these were in South African private collections, others were to be sourced – loans and purchases – in England. It was hoped that this exemplary exhibition would find a permanent home after its closing, to continue as a place of interest and education, a kind of mini colonial Victoria and Albert Museum (V&A).

Florence was given a mandate by the organising committee to source works in England while she was there for her daughter's coming out in May 1909. Any hopes she may have had for securing loans of original items from the V&A were dashed, although she managed to obtain photographs of furniture. The V&A appears to have been rethinking their policy of lending items to the colonies because of the damage incurred, and decreed the following year that all such loans would cease.[19] She felt she was getting nowhere and confided her woes to Caroline Grosvenor who was staying with her at Tylney Hall in April 1909. Enter Hugh Lane. Grosvenor said she knew just the person who could help her, telegraphed Lane, and he arrived the next day. He immediately and completely captivated Florence, so much so that one could say the Johannesburg Art Gallery grew out of her infatuation with Lane. How else can one explain that in the space of two days Lane persuaded her to abandon the arts and crafts museum idea in favour of a gallery of modern art, whisked her up to London to see Philip Wilson Steer's exhibition at the Goupil Gallery and persuaded her to buy the first three paintings for the collection: Steer's *A Chelsea Window*, *Corfe Castle* and *The Lime-Kiln*.[20]

Florence now started seeking funds for a gallery of modern art from the Randlord mining magnates, and Lane started looking for artworks. A major stumbling block, however, was that the canny Randlords would not part with money until they were assured there was a place to house a collection. When Florence set sail for South Africa in early November 1909 she had been promised more than £20,000 but it hadn't materialised, and Lane had already spent £6,000,[21] no doubt from Lionel's pocket. Finding accommodation was critical, for Lionel's finances if nothing else, but the town council only made a firm commitment in mid-1910 to provide temporary accommodation for a collection and to match a donation from the government for the purpose of building an art gallery. Fortunately, Otto Beit had come to the rescue in late 1909, other Randlords gradually contributed funds, and by May 1910 Lane had assembled a large enough collection to display at the Whitechapel Art Gallery. There were further additions and, by the time the collection of just over 130 items was despatched to South Africa in early September 1910, it constituted a remarkably concise and comprehensive representation of British and European modern art and its historical precedents. Lane had achieved this in less than eighteen months.

The collection was opened by the Duke of Connaught in temporary premises at the South African School of Mines and Technology on 29 November 1910. There are no photographic records of how it was displayed, but it is likely the installations followed the categories recorded in the accompanying 1910 catalogue: British Painters, French Painters (Romantic and Barbizon), French Impressionist School, Italian Painters, Portraits (Nucleus of a National Portrait Gallery), Statuary, Etchings, Water-colours and Drawings.[22] There were no South African painters; local efforts were not considered museum material.[23] A comprehensive exhibition of Lane's collection was recreated at the Johannesburg Art Gallery in 2014, following as closely as possible the divisions in the original catalogue, of which a facsimile reprint was published. The installation was compelling in its cohesion and beauty, with Modern British and French Impressionist paintings, and Rodin's marble bust of Miss Eve Fairfax, being particular highlights.

There are two anomalies in the 1910 catalogue that need to be clarified. The first is an entry for Augustus John's *The Family Group*, which did not form part of the Johannesburg Art Gallery's collection. It was lent from Lane's own collection (it is today in Dublin City Gallery The Hugh Lane), because John had not delivered on time the panels for JAG that had been commissioned from him in late 1909 – in fact, he never completed nor delivered them.[24] The second is a catalogue entry for William Orpen's portrait of Otto Beit which had barely been started in 1910 and was only completed in 1913. Orpen informed Robert Ross (who had taken over as honorary director from Lane) in a letter of 9 June 1913 that he had completed the portrait, penning the well-known rhyme, 'The Song of Dublin':

> Committee – We're looking for money
> For Manet and Monet
> Subscribers – And if we get any
> For Monet and Manet
> Will that put an ending
> To Lane and his lending?[25]

At the time the collection was opened by the Duke of Connaught on 29 November 1910, Edwin Lutyens was aboard the *Saxon* sailing to South Africa.[26] Hugh Lane had summoned him by telegram the previous month to come to Johannesburg to design an art gallery and a memorial for the Rand Regiments who had perished in the South African war. Lutyens was in Rome when the summons came, planning the British Pavilion for Rome's International Exhibition of 1911. He was persuaded to accept the offer, and set sail from Southampton on 19 November. By the time he set sail, the Duke of Connaught had already laid the foundation stone for the memorial that was still to be designed, and he probably would have laid a foundation stone for the Johannesburg Art Gallery if its location had been decided. Lutyens enthusiastically engaged with Johannesburg society and council structures, treating them to his usual boyish humour and arrogance. He was not entirely a success and managed to irritate a number of people, like Howard Pim, a prominent citizen, whom he asked if he had any pimples.[27] He also pontificated on what sort of architecture was suitable for South Africa, ignoring the competence of local architects by suggesting that a true South African architecture was still to come.[28]

When it became evident he was likely to be appointed, there was growing resentment from the Association of Transvaal Architects, hardly helped by the municipal council's general inactivity in responding to their queries and complaints. Their protest meeting in February 1911, acrimonious exchanges of letters in the press, council meetings – all attest to the opposition to the appointment of a foreign architect, the fact that there was no competition, and the deception of the donors who now claimed that a condition of their gift was the appointment of an architect of their choice.[29] Lutyens was officially appointed only because the mayor used his casting vote to support him at a 'lively' meeting of 26 April 1911[30] and that was on condition that a local architect, Robert Howden, would supervise the building plans, with Herbert Baker as honorary advisor.[31]

The southern end of Joubert Park was chosen as the gallery's site and Lutyens delivered plans for the laying of the foundation stone on 11 October 1911 and working drawings in 1912. His designs show a remarkable affinity to the classical style of architecture – which he thought was appropriate for a New Country – that he was sketching for his British Pavilion in Rome.[32] The designs for Dublin are less imposing, although similar features like the pedimented niches occur in the design for bridging the Liffey, c.1912. Unfortunately, Dublin Corporation rejected Lutyens as the architect in September 1913.[33]

Lutyens' designs for the Johannesburg Art Gallery were never fully realised. Only the southern main gallery and northward projecting side wings were completed in September 1915; the northern gallery enclosing the central courtyard and the four pavilions projecting to east and west were not built. The Lutyens building opened without ceremony in November 1915.[34] Florence Phillips refused to attend the opening for reasons 'of a deep and serious nature, touching questions of great importance to the public of Johannesburg'. She set out her complaints in a long and bitter open letter to the mayor and the press, the principal in a long list of grievances being the incomplete building.

The large entrance hall, 1930

All due, she claimed, to the town council's lack of interest and obduracy.[35] Lack of interest and funding from the municipal council is a leitmotif that recurs frequently throughout JAG's history.

Fortunately, enough municipal interest was shown during the 1930s to approve the addition built from 1938 to 1940 of the south-west and south-east pavilions, erected according to plans that Lutyens had adapted from his original designs. After delays during 1940 due to wet weather, among other reasons, the pavilions – like the opening of the central section in November 1915 – appear to have opened without ceremony in mid-1941.[36]

Despite not being completed according to the original plans, Lutyens' Johannesburg Art Gallery building presents an extraordinarily beautiful classical façade in a scaled-down grand manner.[37] The details are meticulously designed and coordinated, with adjacent elaborate niches balancing the imposing portal, and the pavilions creating elegant extensions on either side. The interior spaces are as detailed in their design, with a marked sensitivity to the needs of an art gallery. The large entrance hall with its vast decorated ceilings and three large windows presents a perfect well-lit setting for sculpture and furniture. It is flanked by two side galleries with top-lighting, appropriate for displaying paintings. A small apse on either side of the great hall links the three exhibition spaces, creating a squat U-shape plan. These three galleries and two apses were the only parts of Lutyens' original plan that were opened in 1915. Teak is used for doors, windows and skirtings throughout and plaster consoles, which echo the elaborate stone swags and consoles above the entrance door, flank each internal door and support a continuous architrave. The later pavilions are set below the level of the main galleries and are reached by staircases with subtly curved lower steps. They show similar attention to detail as elsewhere in the building, particularly in the stone lobbies linking the old with the new. Along the south façade the pavilions project forward, balancing the grand entrance portal and steps. The details and balance of Lutyens' design, the restrained grandeur, make this one of his most important and beautiful public institutions.

Unfortunately, similar praise cannot be given to the extensions designed by Meyer Pienaar and Partners Inc which opened in 1986. The design was intended to be in the footsteps of Lutyens, to metaphorically complete the Lutyens design by closing off the north façade and echoing the side pavilions. Although there are beautiful features – particularly in the way the two buildings are connected in the central courtyard – the Meyer Pienaar building has become increasingly problematic with

Courtyard linking Lutyens' building with 1986 extensions

inadequate draining, flooding and other structural problems. Large parts of the building today are unusable for exhibitions.

The Lutyens part of the gallery, however, has stood the test of time and, a century after it opened, remains as solid, efficient and beautifully designed as Lutyens had intended.

ENDNOTES

1   The formal opening/donation dates are given. In the case of The Michaelis Collection of seventeenth-century Dutch and Flemish paintings, the legal date of the gift to the Union of South Africa is 16 May 1914 but the collection was placed on public display only in October 1916 and formally inaugurated 8 May 1917. Lane had collated and sold the collection to Max Michaelis nearly five years earlier in November 1912 (J. Carman, *Seventeenth-century Dutch and Flemish Paintings in South Africa: a checklist of paintings in public collections* (Johannesburg, 1994), 12; J. Carman, *Uplifting the Colonial Philistine: Florence Phillips and the making of Johannesburg Art Gallery* (Johannesburg, 2006), 135; M. Stevenson, 'History of the collection' in H. Fransen, *Michaelis Collection, The Old Town House, Cape Town: catalogue of the paintings and drawings* (Zwolle, 1997), 29-43).

2   For a discussion of Lane's two South African collections and Florence Phillips's involvement in their founding see T. Gutsche, *No Ordinary Woman: The life and times of Florence Phillips* (Cape Town, 1966). For the founding of the Johannesburg Art Gallery, see Carman, *Uplifting the Colonial Philistine*.

3   One could argue that the French Impressionist works were not particularly modern, but they were considered exceptional because British institutions did not collect them.

4   S. Koven, 'The Whitechapel picture exhibitions', in D.J. Sherman and I. Rogoff (eds), *Museum Culture* (London, 1994), 28.

5   M. Hardie, 'The world of art: Whitechapel Art Gallery', *The Queen*, 28 May 1910.

6   For a general discussion of reactions in the press, see Carman, *Uplifting the Colonial Philistine*.

7   C.L. Hind, ' Nucleus of a new gallery. Wonderful pictures at Whitechapel', *Evening News*, 13 May 1910.

8   For a comparison of the two collections, see Carman, *Uplifting the Colonial Philistine*, Appendix B.

9   R.F. Foster, '"A family affair"', in B. Dawson (ed.), *Hugh Lane: founder of a gallery of modern art for Ireland* (London, 2008), 19.

10 Carman, *Uplifting the Colonial Philistine*.

11 A formal art gallery committee, to which he would have been accountable, did not exist when Lane was collating Johannesburg's collection, whereas Dublin had a committee that had been formed in December 1904 (Foster, '"A family affair"', 19). Although Lane appears to have had complete curatorial authority, he complains in his Prefatory Notice to the 1910 Johannesburg Art Gallery catalogue, 'I should like to say here that I am not responsible for the choice of a few of the pictures in the Gallery, the inclusion of which I regret'.

12 For example, William Butler Yeats, a close friend of Lane's and a key figure in the literary movement, attended a meeting of the Transvaal Committee (formed in 1899 in support of the Boers) which voted to give the Boer leader Paul Kruger the freedom of Dublin (R.F. Foster, *W.B. Yeats: A Life, I* (Oxford, 1997), 240). Also see A. Wessels, 'The rhetoric of conflict and conflict by rhetoric: Ireland and the Anglo-Boer War (1899-1902)', *Literator*, vol. 20, no. 3 (1999), 161-74.

13 Moore, quoted in R. O'Byrne, *Hugh Lane 1875-1915* (Dublin, 2000), 58.

14 These were the main protagonists, but people of other nationalities, particularly the pro-Boer Irish, also took part in the war and local black people were drawn into the conflict, their role not fully acknowledged in early accounts.

15 Carman, *Uplifting the Colonial Philistine*, 97-98.

16 Charles van Onselen explores the seedy underbelly in his two seminal books on the period: *Studies in the Social and Economic History of the Witwatersrand, I: New Babylon* (Johannesburg, 1982), and *II: New Nineveh* (Johannesburg, 1982)

17 The Jameson Raid of 29 December 1895 to 2 January 1896 was a fabricated and botched attempt to 'rescue' disenfranchised British citizens in Johannesburg and thus gain control of the town. The principal plotters, Lionel included, received death sentences in 1896 which were commuted to prison terms and then fines with a pledge not to participate in politics. Lionel broke his pledge and was

served with a banning order. For a summary description of the events see Carman, *Uplifting the Colonial Philistine*, 272, note 37.

18 An intriguing comparison can be made with Emily Hobhouse's handwork initiatives among young Boer women, to provide occupation and income on farms that had been devastated by the British during the war (J. Carman, 'Arts and Crafts and reconstruction', *Social Dynamics*, vol. 30, no. 1 (2004), 114-40; and 'The users of lace: a socio-political case study', *Image and Text*, vol. 23 (2014), 93-109).

19 'On the 23rd August 1910 (10/3055 M.), Mr. Runciman decided that no original objects, whether belonging to the permanent collections or the Circulation, should ever be lent abroad' (V&A Minute paper, Regd.No. 13/1333).

20 The popular rumour, disseminated by Caroline Grosvenor and Lady Gregory, that she sold her blue diamond ring to finance these purchases is, unfortunately, not true, although she could have used the ring as surety until Lionel, who was currently at sea, arrived in London to settle the bill (Carman, *Uplifting the Colonial Philistine*, pp.111-20; Lady Gregory, *Hugh Lane's Life and Achievement* (London, 1921), 142-44).

21 Gutsche, *No Ordinary Woman*, 236.

22 JAG catalogue, 1910; Carman, *Uplifting the Colonial Philistine*, Appendix D.

23 J. Carman, 'Acquisition policy of the Johannesburg Art Gallery…1909-1987', *South African Journal of Cultural and Art History*, vol. 2, no. 3 (1988), 203-13.

24 In a letter to John Quinn, 25 October 1909, John writes: 'There's a millionairess from Johannesburg who proposes sending me abroad to study and do some decorations for a gallery at Johannesburg which she is founding. If she is sufficiently impressed by what I will show her all will be well. I am extremely anxious to study Italian frescos as I am fired with the desire to revive that art' (New York Public Library, John Quinn Memorial Collection, Reel A1).

25 William Orpen to Robert Ross, 9 June 1913: 'Sorry to worry you but I have finished a picture of one Otto Beit and he has asked me to write to you about having it framed' (JAG, G152).

26 See J. Carman, 'Lutyens in Joubert Park' in T. Murinik (ed.), *Constructure: 100 Years of the JAG Building and its evolution of space and meaning* (Johannesburg, 2016); A. Hopkins and G. Stamp (eds), *Lutyens Abroad: the work of Sir Edwin Lutyens outside the British Isles* (London: The British School at Rome, 2002) and M. Miller, 'City beautiful on the Rand: Lutyens and the planning of Johannesburg' in Hopkins and Stamp, *Lutyens Abroad*, for Lutyens' visit and commissions in South Africa.

27 J. Ridley, *Edwin Lutyens: his life, his wife, his work* (London, 2003), 199.

28 See, for example, the interview in *Rand Daily Mail,* 21 December 1910.

29 Carman, *Uplifting the Colonial Philistine*, 243-52 and Gutsche, *No Ordinary Woman*, 267-69.

30 *Rand Daily Mail*, 27 April 1911.

31 M. McTeague, 'The Johannesburg Art Gallery', *The International Journal of Museum Management and Curatorship*, vol. 3, no. 2 (1984), 143.

32 C. Hussey, *The Life of Sir Edwin Lutyens* (Woodbridge: Antique Collectors' Club, 1989. Reprint of 1950 Country Life edition.), 208-09; M. Miller, 'City beautiful on the Rand'. The British Pavilion was designed for the International Exhibition in Rome, 1911, and formed the basis for the subsequent British School at Rome. Lutyens' 1910 preliminary sketches and plan for the British Pavilion (RIBA Library Drawings Collection [250] 2) are reproduced in H. Hobhouse, '"An architect animated by the spirit of his subject"', in Hopkins and Stamp, *Lutyens Abroad*, 29, fig.12.

33 B. Dawson, 'Hugh Lane and the origins of the collection', in B. Dawson (ed.), *Images and Insights* (Dublin, 1993), 26-27.

34 McTeague, ' The Johannesburg Art Gallery', 143.

35 *The Star*, 30 October 1915.

36 Council minutes for the period 26 March 1940 to 27 May 1941 record the completion of the extensions but do not mention an opening,

37 A.S.G. Butler, with G. Stewart and C. Hussey, *The Lutyens Memorial. The Architecture of Sir Edwin Lutyens. Vol. 2* (Woodbridge, 1989) gives detailed descriptions and photographs of the building. Also see Carman, 'Lutyens in Joubert Park'.

Bibliography

Thomas Bodkin, *Hugh Lane and His Pictures*, Dublin, 1932; reprinted 1956.

Jillian Carman, *Uplifting the Colonial Philistine: Florence Phillips and the making of the Johannesburg Art Gallery*, Johannesburg, 2006.

Catalogue of Pictures Presented to the City of Dublin to Form the Nucleus of a Gallery of Modern Art- Also Pictures Lent by the Executors of the Late Mr J. Staats Forbes and Others, Exhibited at the Royal Hibernian Academy, Dublin 1904.

Catalogue of Pictures Given to the City of Dublin to Form the Nucleus of a Gallery of Modern Art Exhibited at the National Museum, Dublin, 1905.

Catalogue of Pictures Lent to the City of Dublin to form the Nucleus of a Gallery of Modern Art Exhibited at the National Museum, Dublin, 1905.

Barbara Dawson (ed.), *Hugh Lane Founder of a Gallery of Modern Art for Ireland*, Dublin, 2008.

First Exhibition of Modern Paintings, Municipal Art Gallery, Belfast, 1906.

Roy Foster, *W.B. Yeats: A Life, vol. 1, The apprentice image 1865-1914*, Oxford, 1997.

Lady Gregory, *Hugh Lane's life and achievement, with some account of the Dublin galleries*, London, 1921.

Lady Gregory, *Hugh Lane: His Life and Legacy*, New York, 1973.

Sarah Cecilia Harrison, *Municipal Gallery of Modern Art: illustrated Catalogue with bibliographical and critical notes*, Dublin, 1908.

Anne Helmreich and Pamela Fletcher (eds.), *The rise of the modern art market in London, 1850-1939*, Manchester, 2011.

Christopher Hussey, *The Life of Sir Edwin Lutyens,* Woodbridge, 1989.

Hugh Lane, 'Prefactory notice', *Municipal Gallery of Modern Art Illustrated Catalogue,* Johannesburg, 1910.

Loan Exhibition of Modern Paintings Lent by Sir Hugh Lane, Belfast Public Art Gallery and Museum, 1913.

Lucy McDiarmid, *The Irish Art of Controversy,* Dublin, 2005.

Peter Newall, *Cunard Line: a fleet history,* 2012.

Robert O'Byrne, *Hugh Lane, 1875-1915,* Dublin, 2000.

Sylvie Patry (ed.), *Inventing Impressionism: Paul Durand-Ruel and the Modern Art Market,* London, 2015.

James Pethica (ed.), *Lady Gregory's Diaries, 1892-1902,* Oxford, 1996.

John J. Reynolds (ed.), *Statement of the Claim for the Return to Dublin of the 39 Lane Bequest Pictures Now at the Tate Gallery, London,* Dublin, 1932.

Simon Reynolds, *The Vision of Simeon Solomon,* Stroud, 1985.

Jane Ridley, *Edwin Lutyens: his life, his wife, his work,* London, 2003.

G.M. Seymour, *The Life and work of Simeon Solomon (1840-1905),* Santa Barbara, 1986.

Tribute to Sir Hugh Lane, Cork, 1961.

Contributors

DR JILLIAN CARMAN is Visiting Research Associate, Wits School of Arts, University of the Witwatersrand, South Africa.

DR CAROLYN CONROY is an art historian currently affiliated to the University of York and edits the online Simeon Solomon Research Archive.

DR BARBARA DAWSON is Director of Dublin City Gallery The Hugh Lane.

ROY FOSTER is Emeritus Professor of Irish History at the University of Oxford and Professor of Irish History and Literature at Queen Mary University of London.

DR SINÉAD FURLONG-CLANCY is an independent art historian and lecturer.

DR LYNDA MULVIN is Associate Professor, School of Art History and Cultural Policy, University College, Dublin.

ROBERT O'BYRNE is a writer and lecturer specialising in the fine and decorative arts.

JESSICA O'DONNELL is Head of Education and Community Outreach at Dublin City Gallery The Hugh Lane.

DR MORNA O'NEILL is Associate Professor of Art History in the Art Department at Wake Forest University. She is currently writing a book on Hugh Lane and the relationship between the art market and the art museum in the early twentieth century.

Images: © Dublin City Gallery The Hugh Lane except
© The National Gallery, London. Sir Hugh Lane Bequest,
1917, front cover and pp. 6, 14, 17, 45, 80; Courtesy of NIVAL,
National College of Art and Design, Dublin, pp. 54, 56, 58;
© Mark Samuels Lasner Collection, University of Delaware
Library, p. 78; © The National Gallery of Art, Washington, D.C.,
p. 85; © Chrysler Museum of Art, Norfolk, Virginia,
p. 78; © Metropolitan Museum of Art, New York, p. 87, 91;
© Wallace Collection, London, p. 88; © Courtesy of National
Library of Ireland, p. 94; photographs: David Ceruti, pp. 104, 106.

Front cover:
Auguste Renoir *Les Parapluies* (detail)
c. 1881–6
Oil on canvas, 180.3 x 114.9 cm
Sir Hugh Lane Bequest, 1917
© The National Gallery, London

Back cover: Black and white photograph of Sir Hugh Lane, 1913

Editors: Barbara Dawson and Jessica O'Donnell
Copy editor: Elizabeth Mayes
Book design: VERMILLON
Printing: Castuera

ISBN 978-1-901702-51-4
Dublin City Gallery The Hugh Lane
Charlemont House, Parnell Square North,
Dublin 1, Ireland
T: +353 1 2225550
www.hughlane.ie

HUGH LANE
dublin

Comhairle Cathrach
Bhaile Átha Cliath
Dublin City Council